PACKAGING PRESIDENTS
200 YEARS OF CAMPAIGNS & CANDIDATES

Illustrated with selections from the Merrill C. Berman Collection

Essays by

Frederick Voss, Rick Beard & Michael Cheney

Published by

ABRAHAM LINCOLN
PRESIDENTIAL LIBRARY
FOUNDATION

Springfield, Illinois

2008

Packaging Presidents.

Copyright 2008 by the Abraham Lincoln Presidential Library Foundation.

Object photography by Jim Frank

Designed by Steve Hartman, Creativille

The Library of Congress Cataloguing-in-Publication Data
has been applied for.

ISBN: 978-0-97999182-1-60-9799182-1-9

This book was published to accompany *Packaging Presidents:
Two Hundred Years of Campaigns and Candidates*, an exhibition
at the Abraham Lincoln Presidential Library and Museum
from February 5 through November 30, 2008.

Unless otherwise noted in captions or credit lines, all illustrations
in this book are from the Merrill C. Berman Collection.

Table of Contents

Foreword

Packaging Presidents: Two Hundred Years of Campaigns and Candidates REPRISES A PROJECT FIRST COMPLETED IN A MORE MODEST FASHION 24 YEARS AGO. IN 1984, THE HUDSON RIVER MUSEUM IN YONKERS, NEW YORK, HOSTED AN EXHIBITION AND PUBLISHED A MODEST CATALOGUE OF THE SAME TITLE. THEN, AS NOW, THE CORE OF THE EXHIBITION WAS THE COLLECTION OF MERRILL BERMAN, AND THE CURATOR AND PRIMARY AUTHOR WAS FREDERICK VOSS. SIX ELECTIONS AND FOUR PRESIDENCIES LATER, THE SUBJECT HAS LOST NONE OF ITS FASCINATION. THE ESSAYS IN THIS BOOK EXAMINE THEMES THAT HAVE BEEN A PERSISTENT PRESENCE IN AMERICAN PRESIDENTIAL POLITICS FOR NEARLY TWO CENTURIES.

The material remnants of presidential campaigning are today less varied than a century ago, and as often driven by commercial motive as genuine political passion. Television and the Internet have supplanted the buttons, banners, and bandannas of the nineteenth and first half of the twentieth centuries as a means of reaching the electorate. But the themes illustrated so compellingly in the following pages continue to animate our national discussion when electing a president. Forging a connection with the "common man"—whoever he or she might be—is still an essential part of campaigning, leading to embarrassing moments for Republicans and Democrats alike. As Vietnam veterans exit the political scene, the ability to project toughness in the face of America's enemies has replaced direct military experience as a second *sine qua non* in runs for the White House. Our history, however, suggests that this represents no more than a temporary hiatus: in the coming decades, the Iraq War will surely spawn its share of presidential contenders.

Slurs, smears, and personal attacks have been a part of presidential campaigns since 1800. While such forays into political destruction are today often more subtle, and more likely delivered by surrogates rather than the candidates themselves, they remain an effective tool. Indeed, the 24/7 news cycle that characterizes television and the growing reliance upon the Internet have combined to make personal attacks more effective: often without an identifiable source, they reach a far broader audience than was previously the case. *Packaging Presidents* serves as a valuable reminder that, at least in presidential politics, the more things change, the more they stay the same.

This publication was made possible by the efforts of many. Thanks go first to Merrill Berman, who generously shared his extraordinary collection. As the interview published here suggests, great collectors begin early and never lose the passion that animated their initial interest. Informed by an unerring eye for the graphically compelling and the historically illuminating, Merrill has assembled one of the nation's premier collections of presidential memorabilia. A lifetime of collecting such as his serves as a reminder that there is no substitute for the creative individual with a commitment to the authentic artifact.

Jim Frank, who has worked closely with Merrill Berman to catalogue and document the collection for many years, was responsible for the photography on these pages. Frederick Voss, retired Chief Historian for the National Portrait Gallery, Smithsonian Institution, has for many years interpreted the history of presidential campaigning in exhibitions and publications, always with a flair for the unusual tale and a depth and sophistication of understanding that is matched by very few. Dr. James Cornelius, Curator of the Lincoln Collection at the Abraham Lincoln Presidential Library and Museum, and Dr. Erin Bishop, ALPLM Director of Education, provided careful editing of the texts, while Trina Weinert, my executive assistant, braved the world of rights and reproductions to gather the illustrative material not included in the Berman Collection.

Rick Beard
President & CEO
Abraham Lincoln Presidential Library Foundation

COLLECTING AMERICA'S POLITICAL PAST

An Interview with Merrill Berman

Historian Frederick Voss sits down with collector Merrill Berman

Q: After looking over your collection of memorabilia from past presidential campaigns, the first question has to be, "How did you ever get started on this massive undertaking?"

A: Well, my parents were antique collectors. We lived in Newton, just outside Boston, and I can remember when I was maybe five or six going out with them to small New England towns to look for antiques. We'd trudge through one musty shop after another, and somewhere along the way I guess my own collecting instinct kicked in. The focus on political memorabilia, I think, started with my father, who was active in Democratic politics. He had given the nominating speech for Senator Joe Casey when he ran against Henry Cabot Lodge in 1942, and I sometimes went out with him when he campaigned for candidates. I remember going to a convention at the Mechanics Building in Boston. It was an exciting event, and there was lots of campaign memorabilia—buttons, ribbons, whatever—strewn around. On one level, I was attracted to these items simply as souvenirs of political outings with my father. But, by junior high school, I had acquired a graphic sensibility because of my interest in printing and graphic arts. So somehow the design embedded in these campaign buttons and posters attracted me.

Q: So, as a budding collector of campaign ephemera, how did you go about your collecting?

A: Well, Boston got a lot of heavy snowstorms, and I used to go out with my friend to shovel sidewalks and driveways. For doing four or five driveways, we'd make something like twenty-five bucks, and for kids of twelve or so, that was huge.

Then, we'd catch a streetcar into Boston and go to the coin and stamp shops on Bromfield Street. My friend used his share of our earnings to buy stamps for his stamp collection. But some of the dealers also had presidential campaign memorabilia—old celluloid buttons, medals, and ferrotypes—and I began to find it quite satisfying to spend my own money on this kind of stuff.

Q: Do you remember what some of the first items were? If not the first, at least what some of the first items were that you purchased?

A: I'd say they were more tokens and medals from the nineteenth century along with some occasional political buttons from more recent elections—nothing super rare. But that changed when my parents took me to the New Netherlands Coin Company in New York, where I saw some spectacular ferrotype campaign pins, and they weren't cheap. I remember a great two-sided ferrotype from Ulysses Grant's presidential campaign of 1868 with an image of him on one side and on the other an image of his running mate Schuyler Colfax for something like twenty-two dollars. And then there was a really good Lincoln ferrotype from the 1860 campaign *(fig. 1)*. I'm not sure what year that was, but I'll never forget how excited I was to see this higher-quality material.

Lincoln ferrotype, 1860 (fig. 1)

Q: And did you buy some of those higher quality pieces?

A: Well, not exactly. My mother bought the Grant/Colfax for me, I think, as a birthday gift. But most of the time I just kept picking up the more common memorabilia at the shops in Boston for a buck or two or at local campaign headquarters. But not long after that my collecting range expanded considerably when someone, my mother I think, put me onto the American Political Item Collectors, a newly formed group that brought me in contact with a whole network of political memorabilia dealers and collectors. But maybe the biggest breakthrough in my early collecting came when I stumbled across Sam Hoffman, a dealer in Philadelphia. I still have a lot of the things I got from him. He'd go to all the political conventions and scavenge memorabilia by the carton load and he'd send you large boxes full of pins and ribbons from, say, the Republican convention of 1952. But the great thing was that he didn't charge very much for them—maybe fifteen dollars for the whole lot.

Q: As you got older, how did your collecting interests change?

A: Well, for a time they became non-existent. By the time I was sixteen I had a pretty good collection for a beginner, but then my interest in building it up any further went dormant. My collecting instincts did not resurface until after I had graduated from Harvard College and Columbia Business School and gotten myself established as a financial analyst in New York. And, when they did revive, I didn't go back to political ephemera. Instead I started to collect post-impressionist and abstract expressionist paintings and managed to build up quite a good collection that included works by Soutine, Gorky, de Kooning, and Pollock. Unfortunately, I got crushed heavily in the stock-market downturn of 1973-74 and ended up having to sell off the paintings just to stay afloat.

Q: So, how did you get back to campaign memorabilia?

A: I guess I'm one of those people who have to be collecting something. If it's not paintings, it's got to be something else, and somehow not long after that I got interested again in political memorabilia. But when I went out looking for the stuff, I was shocked. The campaign ephemera market had completely changed. For one thing, there were a lot more collectors and dealers out there, and the prices had gone up considerably. Still, the material was much more affordable than paintings, and besides it tied into my interest in history and politics. So I began learning my way around this greatly expanded network of dealers, collectors, and mail-order auction houses. And it was really a lot of fun. Suddenly I was thinking to myself, "Jeez, I think I can take my original collection and build something really serious out of it."

But one of the best parts of getting back to campaign memorabilia was the people I met—the dealers and other collectors. It wasn't at all like the New York art world. There was none of that snobbery or know-it-all attitude. They were all just regular people—postmen, school teachers, car dealers.

Q: So, in effect, you picked up where you had left off at age sixteen or seventeen.

A: Well, not exactly. I was pretty much a neophyte again in some respects. I wasn't really that up on the changed values of ephemera. You might say I was a real pigeon, and there were sharp dealers out there who were more than happy to take advantage of that. Yesterday I ran across some receipts for some things I bought back in about 1980, and I thought "My God! How could I have paid those prices?" Suffice it to say, I had to make a few mistakes before learning how to drive a bargain with some of the dealers.

I had some advantages of my own, however. I was always very systematic and had a pretty sure sense of what I was looking for. I was especially interested in pieces with graphic distinction, and I had a good eye for spotting them. For example, I didn't just want a campaign ribbon; I wanted a campaign ribbon with a strong image, interesting typography, and good overall design. In other words, I had my eye out for traits in political ephemera that a lot of other collectors didn't care as much about.

Q: What have been some of your most unexpected finds in political memorabilia?

A: Interestingly enough, one of my most unexpected finds resulted from the breakup of the Soviet Union in the early 1990s. It turns out that the Soviets had squirreled away quite an archive of political ephemera put out by the American Communist Party, and with the breakup of Russia's Communist regime, a good deal of that material came on the market. As a result I was able to get some really choice and rare posters promoting the presidential candidacy of the Communist Party hopeful William Z. Foster *(fig. 2)*.

Q: Was there any key source that you drew on for building your collection?

A: No, not particularly. There were a few block purchases of items from other collectors that greatly enriched my collection. But mostly it was a cumulative process. Inch by inch, you might say, with a flea market here, an antique dealer there.

Q: If you had to pick, say, four items from your collection that are your prize pieces, what would you pick?

A: I've always loved the Lincoln banners, which stand out partly because of who Lincoln was *(fig. 3)*. But some of the Lincoln material is also just stupendously great—their graphics, their condition, everything. I'm also fond of the anti-Jackson "King Andrew" poster from 1832 *(fig. 4)*. The image and typography on that is wonderful.

Workers Party slate of candidates in New York, 1924 (fig. 2)

Banner for the Replublican presidential ticket, 1860 (fig. 3)

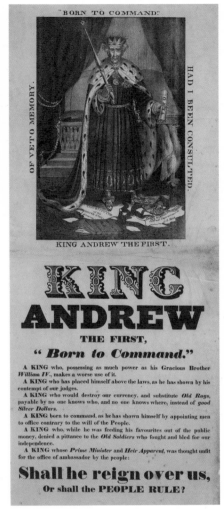

"BORN TO COMMAND."

OF VETO MEMORY.

HAD I BEEN CONSULTED.

KING ANDREW THE FIRST.

KING ANDREW
THE FIRST,
" *Born to Command.*"

A **KING** who, possessing as much power as his *Gracious Brother William IV.*, makes a worse use of it.

A **KING** who has placed himself above the laws, as he has shown by his contempt of our judges.

A **KING** who would destroy our currency, and substitute *Old Rags*, payable by no one knows who, and no one knows where, instead of *good Silver Dollars*.

A **KING** born to command, as he has shown himself by appointing men to office contrary to the will of the People.

A **KING** who, while he was feeding his favourites out of the public money, denied a pittance to the *Old Soldiers* who fought and bled for our independence.

A **KING** whose *Prime Minister* and *Heir Apparent*, was thought unfit for the office of ambassador by the people:

Shall he reign over us,
Or shall the PEOPLE RULE?

Anti-Andrew Jackson broadside, 1832 (fig. 4)

Q: Any other particular favorites?

A: I don't think I'll ever stop being awed by that James K. Polk banner from 1844 *(fig. 5)*. All the embroidery in that piece is amazing. I got that piece from a dealer on Cape Cod, and when I first saw it I just couldn't believe it. Political memorabilia isn't often that elegant. I'm also extremely fond of a large Al Smith button from 1928 that features the images of Smith and his vice-presidential running mate set against Smith's trademark derby hat *(fig. 6)*. Now, that's real punch—really a fantastic graphic! Another great design was the sunflower motif used in the presidential campaign of Kansas governor Al Landon of 1936 *(fig. 7)*. The fact that he happened to come from the sunflower state turned out to be one of the greatest godsends in the whole history of political campaign memorabilia.

Q: Are there any pieces of memorabilia that you'd dearly love to have in your collection that either you couldn't get or that you passed up only to regret doing so?

A: Well, sure, there are bound to be. I have a pin from the campaign of 1864, for example, promoting the candidacy of Democrat George McClellan, and there's a pin done in the same motif that was made for Lincoln in that campaign. I'd love to have that Lincoln mate, but the last time that piece came on the market the asking price was out of this world—running into the many thousands of dollars.

Q: So, rising prices have made going after the rarer and more prized pieces a bit more difficult.

A: A lot more, I'd say. Even the prices for some of the later campaign buttons have gone up astronomically. A really good James Cox/Franklin Roosevelt button from 1920 might run into the many thousands *(fig. 8)*. Collecting political ephemera is definitely no longer a field that a twelve- or thirteen-year-old can easily get into except for the more recent campaign material.

Q: If you were starting out today, would it be possible to build a comparable collection?

A: No. Impossible! At least, I wouldn't be up to it. For one thing, the money required is too large. My collection could've been substantially bigger if I hadn't limited myself to the flat two-dimensional ephemera and gone after the three-dimensional campaign kitsch. Even so, it's pretty big, and given the quality and good condition of so many of the pieces, I think it would be hard to replicate. Even if money were no object, the rarity factor would be a deterrent. You know, the more I think about it, I honestly can't believe that I built this collection. I don't know how I managed to get so many choice pieces. It almost shocks me looking back on it all.

Silk campaign banner for James K. Polk, 1844 (fig. 5)

Al Smith and Joseph Robinson button, 1928 (fig. 6)

Alf Landon Sunflower buttons, 1936 (fig. 7)

James M. Cox and Franklin Roosevelt buttons, 1920 (fig. 8)

BANNERS, BUTTONS & BANDANNAS

REMNANTS OF CAMPAIGNS PAST

Frederick Voss

As I write this opening paragraph

IN MAY OF 2007 ON PRESIDENTIAL ELECTIONS PAST, THE ELECTION OF 2008 IS STILL MANY MONTHS IN THE FUTURE. BUT THE CAMPAIGN LEADING UP TO THAT EVENT HAS BEEN WELL UNDER WAY SINCE JANUARY OF 2007 AND EVEN BEFORE. ON THE REPUBLICAN SIDE, NO FEWER THAN TEN INDIVIDUALS HAVE ANNOUNCED THEIR HOPES OF BECOMING THE GOP'S NEXT WHITE HOUSE STANDARD BEARER, WITH PERSISTENT REPORTS THAT A FEW MORE OF THEIR BRETHREN ARE ON THE SIDELINES, NOT QUITE SURE OF WHEN OR HOW THEY WILL THROW THEIR HAT IN THE RING. MEANWHILE THE RACE FOR THE DEMOCRATIC NOMINATION INCLUDES NO FEWER THAN EIGHT HOPEFULS BUSILY RAISING THE MILLIONS OF DOLLARS NEEDED TO FINANCE THEIR PRESIDENTIAL AMBITIONS AND DAILY HONING THEIR SKILLS IN THE FINE ART OF VOTE-GETTING.

As these White House aspirants go from one rally to another spreading their messages, courting funds, fine-tuning their images, and here and there committing a poorly phrased gaffe that could prove their sudden undoing, the press is on hand to cover and analyze it all. There have already been three televised candidate debates, promptly followed by pundit commentaries evaluating the candidates' performances, and pollsters have been out in full force for months, making their calculations to determine the campaign's front runners. In short, in late May 2007 it seems as if the presidential campaign of 2008 ought by all rights to be drawing to its conclusion. It is hard to believe that it will be well over a year before America's fifty-sixth presidential sweepstakes will finally end.

Presidential electioneering in the United States, however, was not always such a long, drawn-out affair. In the first three decades after the adoption of the Constitution, a presidential election year caused scarcely an up-tick in political activism and speechmaking. In part this resulted from the fact that in many states property-holding and taxpaying requirements sharply curtailed the right to vote, and there were simply not that many voters to be courted. Moreover, as it still does today, the Electoral College ultimately chose the president, and through the election of 1812, a majority of the states chose delegations to that body through their legislatures rather than direct popular vote. But perhaps the major reason for the relative political quiet that characterized early presidential elections lay in the widespread consensus that it was decidedly unseemly for presidential candidates to go about actively seeking votes. The office, it was said, sought the man—not the reverse. As one Congressman put it, the presidency should not be "either solicited or declined," and in 1796, presidential candidate John Adams observed that axiom by sitting out the campaign on his Massachusetts farm while his opponent, Thomas Jefferson, did the same at his beloved Monticello.[1]

The prohibition against presidential aspirants taking to the stump on their own behalf continued to be observed by White House hopefuls through most of the nineteenth century. In 1860, the practice was still held in such low regard that when Democratic hopeful Stephen Douglas launched a speechmaking tour, he felt compelled to claim that his campaign appearances were merely an incidental part of a journey to see his aged mother in rural New York. He, of course, fooled no one, especially in light of the very circuitous route he took to reach his mother's doorstep, and his break from the time-honored rules of presidential candidate decorum deeply offended many. *The New York Times* deemed Douglas's behavior just plain "vulgar" and declared that it was "not a seemly or a welcome sight to see any man who a large portion of his countrymen have thought fit for the Presidency . . . soliciting his own election."[2]

But while the presidential candidates themselves by and large remained aloof from the campaign fray throughout much of the nineteenth century, it did not mean that White House contests continued to retain the subdued character of the country's earliest national elections. By the mid-1820s, the nation's roster of qualified voters had enlarged substantially, thanks both to the admission into the Union of more egalitarian-minded western states that imposed no property-holding or taxpaying restrictions on the right to vote as well as the repeal of such restrictions in many of the older states. The result was that presidential elections became increasingly democratic affairs. In response to that democratization, presidential electioneering gradually took on a more colorful and noisier aspect as candidates' supporters sought to woo and win the rank-and-file electorate by whatever attention-getting means possible.

By the early 1830s involvement in White House contests was fast becoming a sort of communal pastime involving deeply felt loyalties and convictions—equivalent, as one historian has suggested, to the modern-day seasonal enthusiasm for football. Although the French commentator on America's democratic mores, Alexis de Tocqueville, did not stay long enough to see the presidential campaign of 1832 in full swing, his observation on the tenor of American electioneering that he had witnessed the previous year would doubtless have applied to that contest as well. Well before voting day, de Tocqueville said, "the election becomes . . . the all-engrossing topic of discussion. Factional ardor is redoubled, and all the artificial passions which the imagination can create in a happy and peaceful land are agitated."[3]

Among the changes bred by this intensification of voter-wooing and involvement in the late 1820s and the 1830s was an ever increasing outpouring of campaign ephemera, which took many forms, from medals, ribbons, bandannas, and banners to sewing boxes, combs, cartoons, and broadsides. As the years went on, their variety would grow to include such things as walking sticks, watch fobs, soap, and whiskey bottles. But whatever their configuration, they all had one thing in common: emblazoned on them were emblems and slogans, all signifying allegiance to one or another candidate and testifying to the zest and enthusiasm that voters brought to the business of electing their president.

Samuel Johnson once observed that "Life is surely given to us for higher purposes than to gather what our ancestors have wisely thrown away," and a case could be made that the ephemera of past presidential campaigns is precisely the sort of thing to which that bit of wisdom should be applied.[4] After all, once the votes have been tallied, nothing can seem as over and done with as an election, and the campaign ephemera quickly inspire comparisons to a loaf of stale bread. Exhibit "A" is a T-shirt hanging in my own closet, purchased with considerable enthusiasm during the election of 2004, which declared my preference in the contest between George W. Bush and John Kerry. Having been worn only once or twice before Election Day, it is in near mint condition. But I have a hard time conceiving when I will ever wear it again, and if I fail to throw it out, then my heirs certainly will. Or at least that is what I think they should do.

Fortunately for the student of presidential campaigns, not everyone thinks that way, and either out of sheer laziness, sentimental attachment, historical sensibility, or a mixture of all three, the memorabilia of presidential campaigns has been accumulating in American attics, trunks, and corners of jewelry boxes for generations. More important, at some point these pieces became eminently collectible, and as a result, much of that accumulation is preserved today in public museums or private collections.

The motivations behind collecting these political mementoes are many. Some collectors are attracted by their rarity and old, slightly tattered aspect that presents an exotically antique contrast to the clean, unfrayed ephemera of our day. Another attraction may be their design and often richly varied typography. But the main draw of campaign memorabilia, I think, is what it frequently evokes about the colorful human texture and collective participation that vested presidential elections of the past with a kind of carnival-like pageantry. In the vast array of items, for example, that survive from William Jennings Bryan's failed Democratic candidacy of 1896—dinner plates, soap, clocks, mugs, stickpins, handkerchiefs, and much more—one can sense the electrifying impact Bryan had on his followers and the great depth of feeling that characterized his race against William McKinley. Similarly, in the elegant and meticulously stitched fringed banner that a group of unknown women painstakingly embroidered to promote the candidacy of the nation's first dark-horse presidential hopeful, James K. Polk, in 1844, the sense of rank-and-file community involvement in presidential electioneering is almost palpable. Also reflecting the popular texture of the moment is the campaign imagery of Abraham Lincoln from the four-way election of 1860, in which it is possible to see the birth of his rail-splitter persona and how it was already working its way into the American consciousness. And, finally, when one stands back to view the accretion of campaign ephemera from many elections, its colorful critical mass seems to bring to life the observation of British diplomat-statesman James Bryce, who once defined the American presidential contest as a "boom" in which "for three months, processions, usually with brass bands, flags, badges, crowds of cheering spectators, are the order of the day and night from end to end of the country."[5]

The object that could well be entitled to the distinction of being the first bit of ephemera used to promote a presidential candidacy was a metal token manufactured in England and designed to vilify the reputation of Thomas Paine. After galvanizing the American Revolution with his pamphlet *Common Sense* in 1776, Paine went on to participate in the French Revolution and had grown more radical in his egalitarian thinking. In *Rights of Man,* published in 1791, he called for the overthrow of the English monarchy, which led in turn to his conviction *in absentia* for treason in his native Britain. But his extremism did not stop there, and in *The Age of Reason,* he raised challenges to traditional organized religion. As a result, by the mid-1790s, many Americans had come to regard this once honored promoter of American independence as a dangerously subversive atheist. But Paine managed to hang onto at least one friend in America. His name was Thomas Jefferson, and when Jefferson ran for president in 1796 and 1800, the evidence suggests that Jefferson's opponents circulated some of the anti-Paine tokens imported from England in an effort to identify him with Paine's alleged godless extremism.

That oblique bit of negative advertising was but a faint harbinger of things to come, and it was not until the contest of 1828 between John Quincy Adams and Andrew Jackson that the use of promotional mementoes began to set down permanent roots in the presidential campaigning tradition. The campaign of 1828 was one of the longest White House campaigns ever. It began, in fact, with the conclusion of the 1824 presidential contest among Jackson, Adams, William Crawford, and Henry Clay. In popular votes, Jackson had won. But neither he nor any other candidate could claim a majority in the Electoral College, and when the contest, as required by the Constitution, was thrown into the House of Representatives, Adams emerged the winner. Taken by itself, this was bound to cause some bitterness among Jackson's supporters, but their unhappiness was compounded by the fact that Adams had tacitly agreed to make rival candidate Henry Clay his Secretary of State in exchange for Clay's throwing House support to Adams. As a result, from the moment of Adams's election, Jacksonians were raising the cry of "corrupt bargain" and laying plans to avenge this outrageous injustice in 1828.

The burning drive to get even prompted an outpouring of ephemera from both sides to curry favor with voters. Among the items were small medals, pitchers, dinner plates, thread boxes, and combs. In creating vote-getting images for these items, the Jacksonians had a distinct edge, for Jackson had first come to public notice in the War of 1812 as the hard-bitten frontier general who had trounced the British at the Battle of New Orleans. His supporters wasted no time in capitalizing on that battlefield fame, and as often as not the Jackson images produced in 1828 showed him turned out in military dress. Adams's campaign supporters doubtless groused at this ploy, echoing Henry Clay's remark that "killing 2500 Englishmen at New Orleans" hardly qualified anyone for the "difficult and complicated duties of the chief magistracy."[6] That may well have been true. Nevertheless there was no denying that allusions to military prowess had an unusually powerful allure for voters, and perhaps the memento most commonly seen in the campaign of 1828 was a hickory branch brandished by Jackson's followers as a shorthand allusion to the intrepid toughness that had inspired the men under Jackson during the War of 1812 to dub him "Old Hickory."

Adams's supporters, however, did not sit idly by while all the celebrations of Jackson's military prowess worked their spell over the electorate, and they were quickly bending to the task of removing the sheen from Old Hickory's epaulettes. Among their most potent tarnishing agents was a "six coffin" handbill that they passed out featuring examples of Jackson's draconian brand of military justice during the War of 1812, including the tale of how, following the Battle of New Orleans, Jackson had ordered the execution of six of his men found guilty of insubordination *(fig. 1)*. But Jackson's supporters were not to be cowed by this effort to play up their candidate's taste for unnecessary harshness. Instead, unashamedly taking their metaphorical cues from the coffin broadside, they produced a wood engraving showing Adams strung from a gibbet, declaring that "Jackson is to be President, and you will be HANGED."[7]

In the story of presidential campaign memorabilia no White House contest was more memorable than the contest of 1840 between Whig candidate William Henry Harrison and the Democratic incumbent Martin Van Buren. Known as the "Log Cabin Hard Cider" campaign, it owed its name to a remark in a pro-Van Buren newspaper in Baltimore suggesting that Harrison could best serve the interests of the nation by retiring to his log cabin in Ohio and passing his remaining days reading "moral philosophy" between drinks of hard cider. After penning this observation, its author may well have silently congratulated himself on its sardonic wit. But if he did, the congratulations were decidedly premature. When a pair of Whig strategists focused on the remark and pondered the damage it might do as it made the rounds in other Democratic newspapers, they suddenly realized that in this partisan barb lay the seeds of a Whig victory. So it was that a keg of hard cider and a humble log cabin became the emblems of a campaign designed to link Harrison to the rustic virtues and homespun simplicity of the American frontier and in the process identify him with the interests and concerns of rank-and-file voters *(fig. 2)*.

Harrison was not the common man that this imagery suggested. Born into an aristocratic Virginia family, he was the son of a signer of the Declaration of Independence, and his Ohio farmhouse was in fact quite stately. But those inconvenient truths did not matter a whit to his campaign strategists, who embellished his log cabin hard cider persona further by playing up his past as a frontier soldier and heroic victor over a force of Indians at the Battle of Tippecanoe.

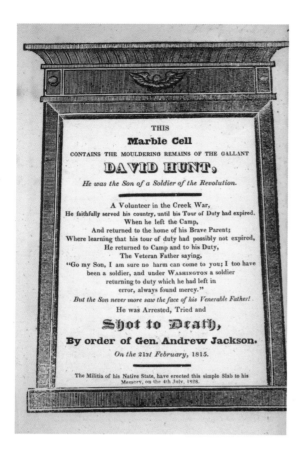

"The Marble Cell . . . of the Gallant David Hunt"

"Within these narrow walls are deposited the mortal remains of John Woods"

Handbills charging Andrew Jackson with undue brutality (fig. 1)

Constant celebration of Jackson's battlefield prowess in the War of 1812 by his supporters in 1828 led his opposition to remind voters of the darker side of his military record. In the two anti-Jackson handbills here, made to look like burial tablets, the electorate learned of incidents in which Jackson had ordered the executions of soldiers—one for desertion and the other for mutiny. The harsh punishments, Jackson's critics claimed, were proof positive that he was little more than an inhumane brute.

Log cabin hard cider emblems from 1840 linking William Henry Harrison to rank-and-file voters (fig. 2)

The main vehicle for promoting this amalgam of homespun virtue and battlefield bravery was a campaign short on addressing public issues and notably long on noisy public demonstrations such as the country had never before witnessed. With this carnival-like brouhaha came an unprecedented flood of campaign mementoes that included large parade banners, more than 20 styles of bandannas, 200 types of ribbons, a vast array of pitchers and plates, and novelty products such as Tippecanoe Tobacco and Tippecanoe Shaving Soap. There was even a whiskey bottle in the shape of a log cabin.

The non-stop celebration of Harrison's rustic virtues and Indian-fighting heroics may have been the Whigs' main vehicle for swaying the electorate of 1840. But there was yet another weapon in the Whigs' campaign arsenal that also proved immensely valuable—the portrayal of White House incumbent Martin Van Buren as an effete dandy with appetites for French perfumes and gilded tableware (fig. 3). The contrast between the homespun Harrison and a sybaritic Van Buren was the perfect ingredient for topping off the Whigs' log cabin brew, and one of the favorite Whig ditties of the day declared:

> Let Van from his coolers of silver drink wine,
> And lounge on his cushioned settee:
> Our man on his buckeye bench can recline,
> Content with hard cider is he![8]

A good many Americans were dumbstruck and even a bit scandalized by the Whig strategy of 1840. Viewing the proceedings from his plantation in Tennessee, ex-President Andrew Jackson called it "humbuggery," and the strategy's chief victim Martin Van Buren would later describe it as the "debaucheries of a political Saturnalia, in which reason and justice had been derided."[9] But, in the wake of Harrison's victory at the polls, no one could dispute its success, and although its raucous character would never quite be equaled in future presidential contests, the campaign of 1840 had set a pattern that was destined to make presidential contests considerably livelier affairs and would unleash a quadrennial flood of ephemera declaring the virtues and vices of the latest crop of White House aspirants.

Four years later, when Whig candidate Henry Clay ran against the Democratic dark horse James K. Polk, the country found itself once again inundated with electioneering mementoes. Among the more noteworthy aspects of that outpouring was the sense of affection implied in so much of the sloganeering found on the Clay ribbons and banners. This is perhaps not so surprising in light of fierce personal attachment that many Whigs had come to feel for Clay. He was their "Gallant Harry," their "Western Star," their "friend of truth, of soul sincere/In action faithful and honor clear." Unfortunately, such heartfelt testaments to Clay's virtues could not a triumph make. In the end, tripped up by his straddling on the issue of admitting Texas to the Union, he lost by a narrow margin to Polk. Of the many times he had sought the presidency, this had been Clay's best chance for achieving it. His loss plunged him into a period of uncharacteristic gloom during which his oft-quoted remark that "I would rather be right than the President" offered scant solace.[10] Maybe that sentiment had some merit, but at the moment it doubtless seemed vastly overrated.

No one would ever argue that the quality and quantity of campaign memorabilia ever became a decisive factor in determining the outcome at the polls. On the other hand, surviving ephemera from White House contests can sometimes offer insights into the electioneering strategies that caused one candidate to win over another. A prime example was the election of 1856, in which John C. Fremont became the presidential candidate of

A BEAUTIFUL GOBLET OF WHITE-HOUSE CHAMPAGNE

AN UGLY MUG OF LOG-CABIN HARD CIDER

Anti-Martin Van Buren memento from the campaign of 1840 (fig. 3)

While William Henry Harrison's supporters portrayed their candidate as a simple man of the people, they delighted in depictions of his opponent, Martin Van Buren, as a champagne-swilling dandy. In the case of the image here, however, a pull of a tab transforms Van Buren the bon vivant into a hapless post-election loser, reduced to toasting the victory of his opponent with a cup of Harrison hard cider.

the Republican Party, the country's newborn political coalition of the anti-slavery movement. In promoting Fremont, his supporters emphasized their abolitionist principles above all else, and the slogan "Free Men, Free Soil, and Fremont" struck the dominant note in just about all of the Republicans' promotional ephemera.[11] But the country—North as well as South—was not ready for such unequivocal trumpeting of opposition to slavery in a national election, and in the end Fremont was defeated.

In ruminating over their loss, a number of Republican strategists saw the connection between Fremont's defeat and the high visibility given in the campaign to their party's anti-slavery position. As a result, when Abraham Lincoln became the Republicans' presidential standard bearer four years later, his supporters were careful to downplay and moderate their anti-slavery views, and only in communities where abolitionist sentiment ran high did they dare to focus on them with any frankness. Not surprisingly, this temporizing on abolitionism was mirrored in the party's promotional memorabilia. In contrast with the sloganeering against slavery seen on Republican banners and ribbons of 1856, the ephemera championing Lincoln's cause alluded to the issue only in the most indirect terms, if at all, and a good deal of its imagery harkened back to the log-cabin strategies of 1840, emphasizing Lincoln's frontier origins and youthful endeavors as a rail-splitter.

While Lincoln's humble beginning was a decided asset in selling his candidacy, he had one attribute that proved somewhat worrisome to his supporters. Lincoln was not a handsome man, and in many lights his coarsely featured face seemed downright homely. To make matters worse, many of the images of him initially circulated to the public following his presidential nomination were based on unflattering photographs *(fig. 4)*. Before long there was an anti-Lincoln song making the rounds that ran in part:

> Tell us of his fight with Douglas—
> How his spirit never quails;
> Tell us of his manly bearing,
> Of his skill in splitting rails
>
> Any lie you tell we'll swallow—
> Swallow any kind of mixture;
> But oh! Don't, we beg and pray you—
> Don't, for God's sake, show his picture.[12]

Clearly this was a problem that needed addressing, and Lincoln spent a good deal of time in the summer of 1860 sitting for likenesses that were intended to show him in a more flattering light and could be used as the basis for campaign prints. Among those involved in this image makeover effort was one Judge John Read of Philadelphia, who dispatched a portraitist to Lincoln's home in Springfield on the understanding that the artist would come back with a picture that was "good looking whether the original justify it or not."[13]

The artist hired by Read, John Henry Brown, succeeded in his assignment to everyone's satisfaction, producing a likeness that Lincoln's secretary declared to be "both very pretty and very truthful." But the artist who deserved first prize in the effort to prettify Lincoln was Charles Barry, who managed to invest the coarseness of his subject's features and the chronic unruliness of his thick hair with a poetically lyrical quality that seemed intent on presenting Lincoln as a kind of American Lochinvar. "The portrait," a much relieved Republican newspaper reported soon after its completion, "will correct the impression . . . derived from . . . the shocking

1857 photograph of Abraham Lincoln, basis of many of his early campaign images (fig. 4)

Of the early portrait images produced to promote Lincoln's presidential candidacy in 1860, one observer speculated that there had to be some sort of a contest afoot to turn him into "the ugliest of men." Some of the images that the writer doubtless had in mind were the many that were based on this photograph by Alexander Hesler showing a tousle-haired Lincoln in a clearly unflattering light.

Abraham Lincoln Presidential Library and Museum

Abraham Lincoln by Charles A. Barry (fig. 5)

Done in the summer of 1860, this drawing of Lincoln invested its subject's homely, rough-hewn features with a romanticized softness. At its unveiling at a Lincoln rally in Massachusetts it met with the "wildest enthusiasm." When translated into the lithograph pictured here, however, the likeness did not sell well, perhaps because its three-dollar asking price put it beyond the reach of most political print consumers of the day.

Abraham Lincoln Presidential Library and Museum

prints which have been made to pass for [Lincoln's] portraits. Truth constrains us to say that 'Honest Abe' is not a handsome man; but he is not so ill-looking as he has been represented."[14] Nor, however, did he have quite the romantic dash that Barry had imparted to him *(fig. 5)*.

In the story of presidential promotional ephemera, campaigns for the nation's highest office have occasionally been marked by their preoccupation with a certain type of memorabilia. That certainly was the case in the contest of 1888 between Grover Cleveland and Benjamin Harrison, which has been dubbed the Battle of the Bandannas. Cleveland's running mate Allen G. Thurman, who always carried a red handkerchief in his hip pocket and routinely pulled it out to shield the inevitable sneeze following one of his frequent pinches of snuff, provided the inspiration for this battle. Shortly after Thurman received the vice-presidential endorsement, an observer quipped that the Democrats had just "nominated a pocket handkerchief."[15] In a manner of speaking, they had indeed, and the opening salvo in the Battle of the Bandannas took the form of a jubilant flurry of red handkerchiefs on the floor of the Democratic convention. With that the bandanna became the unofficial symbol of the Democratic cause. Before long party faithful had their pick of more than a dozen varieties of handkerchiefs signifying their fealty to the Cleveland-Thurman ticket.

Initially, the Republicans looked on the sudden craze for bandannas with disdain, but when they saw how these squares of colorfully printed silk and cotton were stirring the electorate, they began building their own handkerchief arsenal. By election day, when Harrison claimed the White House, it has been estimated that his Republican supporters had outstripped the opposition in bandanna consumption by some thirty percent.

In 1893, a Boston woman named Amanda Lougee received a patent for a metal button covered with a thin piece of transparent celluloid. It was an event destined to have an enduring impact on campaign memorabilia. Shortly thereafter she sold the patent to the Whitehead and Hoag Company in New Jersey, whose proprietors proceeded to turn Lougee's invention into a new vote-getting device by inserting a political candidate's photo image beneath the celluloid and securing both to a cheap metal round backing suitable for pinning on a lapel. The modern campaign button was born. Although the celluloid-covered photograph has long since been displaced by other image-creating means, the campaign pin of today still has the same configuration that it did back in the summer of 1896, when Whitehead and Hoag issued their first buttons for the presidential contest between Republican William McKinley and the Democrats' "Great Commoner," William Jennings Bryan.

By the time McKinley and Bryan faced off against each other, a plenitude of promotional ephemera had long been a predictable element in the rituals of presidential campaigning, and as with anything that becomes predictable, it had doubtless lost some of its vote-getting punch. The McKinley-Bryan election, however, brought forth a tidal wave of campaign objects that added substantially to the color and spirit of the contest.

With parts of the country still suffering from the final throes of the worst economic depression in its history, the White House contest of 1896 struck many as a kind of Armageddon between the forces of light and darkness. With thousands of workers unemployed and many farmers near ruin as a result of falling crop prices, the main issue was how to restore prosperity. For Bryan, the answer was simple: Having electrified the Democratic convention with his declaration that "you shall not crucify mankind upon a cross of gold," he championed an inflationary monetization of silver at a 16 to 1 ratio with gold.[16] For the McKinleyites, however, departure from the gold standard in the nation's currency spelled certain financial disaster with grass growing in streets of every city in the country *(fig. 6)*.

*Novelty card from 1896 contrasting the dire results of a Bryan victory
with the salutary impact of a McKinley victory (fig. 6)*

The debate over gold and silver generated a depth of feeling that expressed itself at least in part by an incredibly strong appetite among voters for mementoes testifying to their loyalty to one side or the other. By election day, the tally of campaign objects produced to promote Bryan and McKinley included one thousand kinds of celluloid buttons, close to one hundred varieties of stickpins, and several hundred different ribbons *(fig. 7)*. But perhaps even more noteworthy was the campaign's rich assortment of other partisan sundries. Whatever the need in one's daily life, it almost seemed that there was a McKinley or Bryan item to meet it. The smoker of 1896 could take his pick of Bryan and McKinley ashtrays and cigar-holders. The hygienically minded could bathe with Bryan or McKinley soap. Republican children could run races with their McKinley dolls in contests where their Democratic playmates could signify the start by blowing on their Bryan "free silver" whistles. Meanwhile their aging grandparents could steady themselves with Bryan or McKinley walking sticks, and those anxious about being on time for an appointment could consult their Bryan or McKinley timepieces.

In the first several decades of the twentieth century, presidential campaign ephemera continued to be a very visible part of the nation's electioneering tradition. With the advent of radio and movie newsreels in the 1920s and 30s, however, its prominence began to ebb, as White House candidates and their managers became focused on ways to use those media for advancing their cause. Nearly disappeared by 1940, if not entirely gone, were the days of local town-square parades and rallies that had once involved voters directly in promoting their candidates and had in the process yielded bumper crops of banners and ribbons.

The advent of television further eroded the use of traditional memorabilia in presidential campaigning. Beginning with the televising of the national party nominating conventions in 1952, voters were now experiencing more and more of the presidential election process in the solitude of their living rooms and dens, and in that isolated setting the impulse to brandish a bandanna or sport a ribbon in support of a candidate declined precipitously. At the same time, television largely preempted campaign memorabilia's selling functions, as election consultants took to filling prime-time viewing hours with slickly packaged fifteen- and thirty-second candidate "spots."

Nevertheless the tradition of slogan- and image-emblazoned mementoes is not entirely dead. As the business of promoting White House hopefuls moves into high gear every four years, Americans can still count on seeing an outpouring of latter-day descendants of the Andrew Jackson thread box, Henry Clay parade banner, and Grover Cleveland bandanna. With the presidential election of 2008 still many months away, I have already spotted a bumper sticker on a neighbor's car declaring allegiance to Rudy Giuliani, and by election day, if the past few presidential campaigns are any indication, I can expect that the front lawns of a hefty percentage of the houses in my neighborhood will be festooned with placards announcing to the world which White House hopeful their inhabitants are intending to support when they draw the curtain behind them in the voting booth. Exactly what effect these pre-election declarations of voter fealty will have on the outcome of 2008 will be difficult to measure. More likely than not, it will be fairly negligible. But one thing is certain: The presence of promotional ephemera will add, as it always has, to the spirit and color that have for so long been the hallmark of this country's presidential contests.

Gold and silver bugs from the campaign of 1896 (fig. 7)

Among the most popular vehicles for showing your presidential preference in 1896 were gold and silver bug-pins. If a voter favored the idea of raising wages and farm prices by monetizing silver, he opted for sporting the pro-Bryan silver bug on his lapel; if he favored sticking to the gold standard, he opted for the pro-McKinley gold bug.

Endnotes

1 "either solicited or declined" in Roger A. Fischer, *Tippecanoe and Trinkets Too: The Material Culture of American Presidential Campaigns, 1828-1984* (Urbana: University of Illinois Press, 1988), p. 2.

2 "vulgar" and "not a seemly or a welcome . . . ." in Robert W. Johannsen, *Stephen A. Douglas* (New York: Oxford University Press, 1973), p. 781.

3 "the election becomes" in Arthur M. Schlesinger, Jr., ed. *Running for President: The Candidates and Their Images* (New York: Simon and Schuster, 1994), xvi.

4 "Life is surely given . . . ." in Samuel Johnson, *Yale Edition of the Works of Samuel Johnson,* vol. IV (New Haven: Yale University Press, 1969), pp. 285-286.

5 "boom" and "for three months . . . ." in Kathleen Hall Jamieson, *Packaging the Presidency* (New York: Oxford University Press, 1984), p. 5.

6 "killing 2500 Englishmen at New Orleans . . ." in Lillian Miller et al., *'If Elected . . .': Unsuccessful Candidates for the Presidency, 1796-1968* (Washington, D.C.: Smithsonian Institution Press, 1972), p. 92.

7 "Jackson is to be President . . . HANGED" caption from wood engraving in the collection of the New-York Historical Society.

8 "Let Van from his coolers . . . ." in Lillian Miller et al., *'If Elected . . .,'* p. 128.

9 "humbuggery" and "debaucheries of a political Saturnalia . . . ." in Roger A. Fischer, *Tippecanoe and Trinkets Too,* pp. 29 and 49.

10 "Gallant Harry," "Western Star," "friend of truth . . .," and "I would rather be right . . . ." in Frederick Voss and Rick Beard, *Packaging Presidents; Memorabilia from Campaigns Past* (Yonkers, NY: The Hudson River Museum, 1984), pp. 13-14.

11 "Free Men, Free Soil, and Fremont" in Roger A. Fischer, *Tippecanoe and Trinkets Too,* p. 72.

12 "Tell us of his fight with Douglas . . ." in Harold Holzer, Gabor S. Boritt, Mark E. Neely, Jr., *The Lincoln Image: Abraham Lincoln and the Popular Print* (New York: Charles Scribner's Sons, 1984), p. 2.

13 "good looking whether the original . . . ." in Holzer et al., *The Lincoln Image,* (New York: Charles Scribner's Sons, 1984), p. 61.

14 "The portrait . . . ." in the *New-York Daily Tribune,* June 11, 1860, p. 5.

15 "nominated a pocket handkerchief" in Roger A. Fischer, *Tippecanoe and Trinkets Too,* p. 132.

16 "You shall not crucify mankind . . ." in Lewis Copeland, Lawrence W. Lamm, Stephen J. McKenna, ed. *The World's Great Speeches,* (Mineola, NY: Dover Publications, Inc., 1999), p. 336.

A New National Pastime

1828-1856

The way in which Americans choose their president underwent several significant changes in the decades immediately after the ratification of the U. S. Constitution. The first of these changes provided for separate voting for president and vice president in the Electoral College. In the first four presidential elections, there was no distinction drawn between the two offices. In 1796 this led to an administration in which the president, John Adams, was a member of the Federalist Party, while his vice president, Thomas Jefferson, owed allegiance to the Democratic-Republican Party. Matters became even more confused four years later, when Jefferson and Aaron Burr received identical numbers of votes in the Electoral College, throwing the election's outcome into the House of Representatives for the first (but not last) time. While Jefferson won the office, the turmoil caused by the muddled political situation led to the adoption of the twelfth amendment in 1804.

Other aspects of presidential electioneering that were not constitutionally mandated also underwent change. In many states property-holding and taxpaying requirements sharply limited the size of the voting public in the young republic. Moreover, through the election of 1812, a majority of the states chose delegations to the Electoral College in their legislatures rather than by direct popular vote, and not until 1824 are there reliable records of the popular vote for president. The absence of America's rank and file citizenry in electing the first presidents ensured that the earliest contests for the nation's highest office were decidedly quiet affairs. The gradual disappearance of these laws greatly enlarged the nation's popular electorate, and by 1828 direct appeals to voters through speechmaking and demonstrations were becoming an ever more crucial element in campaigns for the White House.

By the fourth decade of the nineteenth century, the once subdued business of electing a president had been transformed into a quadrennial pageant that often took on the color and noise of a nationwide carnival. Absent from the festivities were the presidential aspirants themselves, for conventional wisdom deemed it unseemly for candidates to go about actively seeking votes. With very few exceptions, presidential candidates did not begin actively campaigning until the late nineteenth century.

Today that color and noise is played out mostly on television and the Internet in a 24/7 news cycle that would boggle the mind of nineteenth-century campaign strategists. Nevertheless, one of the central aspects of modern-day campaigning—the so-called "packaging" of presidential hopefuls through visual imagery and sloganeering—is a political art form that is rooted in a tradition that goes back some two hundred years. The five photo essays that follow amply demonstrate that a button or broadside from the election of 1828 and the slick television ads of 2008 have considerably more in common than one may initially think.

Election Year	Candidate	Office	Party	Electoral Vote	Popular Vote
1789	George Washington	P		69	
	John Adams	VP		34	
	John Jay			9	
	John Hancock			4	
	Eight Others			22	
1792	George Washington	P		132	
	John Adams	VP		77	
	George Clinton			50	
	Thomas Jefferson			5	
	Aaron Burr			1	
1796	John Adams	P	Federalist	71	
	Thomas Jefferson	VP	Democratic-Republican	68	
	Thomas Pinckney		Federalist	59	
	Aaron Burr		Democratic-Republican	30	
	Samuel Adams		Democratic-Republican	15	
	Oliver Ellsworth		Federalist	11	
	Seven others			22	
1800	Thomas Jefferson	P	Democratic-Republican	73	
	Aaron Burr	VP	Democratic-Republican	73	
	John Adams	P	Federalist	65	
	Charles C. Pinckney	VP	Federalist	64	
	John Jay		Federalist	1	
1804	Thomas Jefferson	P	Democratic-Republican	162	
	George Clinton	VP			
	Charles C. Pinckney	P	Federalist	14	
	Rufus King	VP			
1808	James Madison	P	Democratic-Republican	122	
	George Clinton	VP	Independent-Republican	6	
	Charles C. Pinckney	P	Federalist	47	
	Rufus King	VP			
1812	James Madison	P	Democratic-Republican	128	
	Elbridge Gerry	VP			
	DeWitt Clinton	P	Federalist	89	
	Charles J. Ingersoll	VP			
1816	James Monroe	P	Democratic-Republican	183	
	Daniel D. Tompkins	VP			
	Rufus King	P	Federalist	34	
	Four Candidates				
1820	James Monroe	P	Democratic-Republican	231	
	Daniel D. Tompkins	VP			
	John Quincy Adams	P	Independent-Republican	1	
	Four Candidates				
1824	Andrew Jackson	P	Democratic	99	153,544
	John Calhoun	VP	(ran on both tickets)		
	John Quincy Adams	P	Democratic-Republican	84	108,740
	John Calhoun	VP	(ran on both tickets)		
	William H. Crawford			41	46,618
	Henry Clay			37	47,136

The Grudge Match of 1828

The election of 1828 was a grudge match pitting White House incumbent John Quincy Adams against Andrew Jackson. In the four-way presidential contest four years earlier, Jackson had claimed the largest popular vote. But because none of the candidates could claim a majority in the Electoral College, the election was thrown into the House of Representatives. Thanks in part to some behind-the-scenes deal-making, Adams emerged the winner. A drive for revenge, borne of a belief that a "corrupt bargain" had denied Jackson what had been rightfully his, galvanized a second White House bid.

The Hero of New Orleans

Jackson's fame as the general who had defeated the British at the Battle of New Orleans at the close of the War of 1812 was chief among his selling points in the election of 1828. His supporters never missed an opportunity to remind voters of that glorious moment. While an opponent once groused that "Killing 2500 Englishmen" hardly qualified him for "the difficult . . . duties of the chief magistracy," Jackson's military prowess had great allure for the electorate.

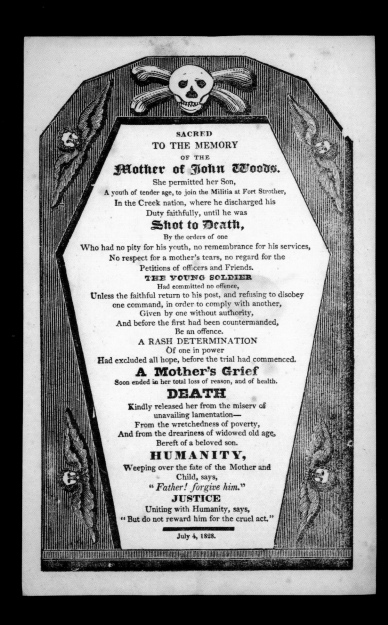

SACRED
TO THE MEMORY
OF THE
Mother of John Woods.
She permitted her Son,
A youth of tender age, to join the Militia at Fort Strother,
In the Creek nation, where he discharged his
Duty faithfully, until he was
Shot to Death,
By the orders of one
Who had no pity for his youth, no remembrance for his services,
No respect for a mother's tears, no regard for the
Petitions of officers and Friends.
THE YOUNG SOLDIER
Had committed no offence,
Unless the faithful return to his post, and refusing to disobey
one command, in order to comply with another,
Given by one without authority,
And before the first had been countermanded,
Be an offence.
A RASH DETERMINATION
Of one in power
Had excluded all hope, before the trial had commenced.
A Mother's Grief
Soon ended in her total loss of reason, and of health.
DEATH
Kindly released her from the misery of
unavailing lamentation—
From the wretchedness of poverty,
And from the dreariness of widowed old age,
Bereft of a beloved son.
HUMANITY,
Weeping over the fate of the Mother and
Child, says,
"Father! forgive him."
JUSTICE
Uniting with Humanity, says,
"But do not reward him for the cruel act."

July 4, 1828.

Tarnishing a Hero

Jackson's political opponents mounted a campaign to tarnish Jackson's soldierly fame. Handbills such as the ones seen here were among their chief weapons, recalling examples of the harsh military justice that Jackson sometimes dealt out during the War of 1812, including the execution of soldiers in situations where the evidence against them may have been questionable.

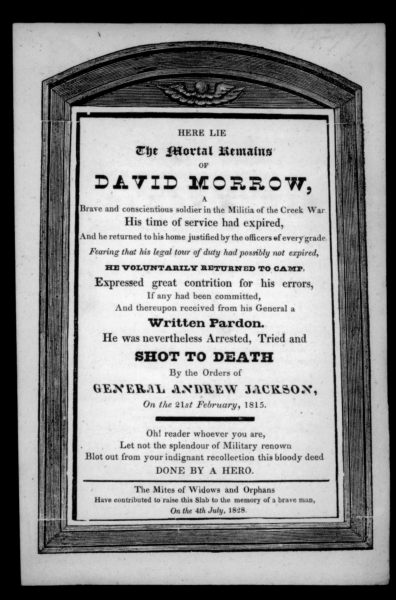

Election Year	Candidate	Office	Party	Electoral Vote	Popular Vote
1828	Andrew Jackson	P	Democratic	178	647,286
	John Calhoun	VP			
	John Quincy Adams	P	National Republican	83	508,064
	Richard Rush	VP			

1832
"King Andrew I"

Following his triumph over Adams, Jackson proved to be every bit as decisive in the White House as he had been as a general, wielding his executive authority with aggressiveness unmatched by any of his predecessors. His expansion of presidential power raised cries of Constitutional usurpation: one broadside published during his bid for a second presidential term in 1832 painted Jackson as a would-be monarch intent on trampling the last vestige of his country's democratic institutions. Jackson's well-deserved reputation for forceful leadership did little to dim his popular appeal. He handily defeated Henry Clay, for whom Jackson had considerable enmity dating back to the 1824 election. William Wirt, attorney general under Presidents James Monroe and John Quincy Adams, ran on the Anti-Masonic ticket, a short-lived party initially established to oppose secret societies that quickly became an anti-Jackson party.

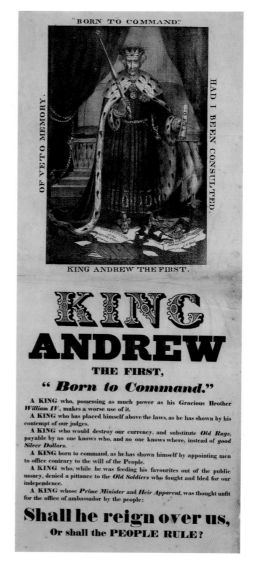

"BORN TO COMMAND."

OF VETO MEMORY.

HAD I BEEN CONSULTED.

KING ANDREW THE FIRST.

KING ANDREW
THE FIRST,
"Born to Command."

A **KING** who, possessing as much power as his *Gracious Brother William IV.*, makes a worse use of it.

A **KING** who has placed himself above the laws, as he has shown by his contempt of our judges.

A **KING** who would destroy our currency, and substitute *Old Rags,* payable by no one knows who, and no one knows where, instead of *good Silver Dollars.*

A **KING** born to command, as he has shown himself by appointing men to office contrary to the will of the People.

A **KING** who, while he was feeding his favourites out of the public money, denied a pittance to the *Old Soldiers* who fought and bled for our independence.

A **KING** whose *Prime Minister* and *Heir Apparent*, was thought unfit for the office of ambassador by the people:

Shall he reign over us,
Or shall the PEOPLE RULE?

Campaign Results

Election Year	Candidate	Office	Party	Electoral Vote	Popular Vote
1832	Andrew Jackson	P	Democratic	219	701,780
	Martin Van Buren	VP			
	Henry Clay	P	National Republican	49	484,205
	John Sargeant	VP			
	John Floyd		Nullifer	11	100,715
	William Wirt		Anti-Masonic	7	—
	Others			—	7,273

1836
The Election of the "Little Magician"

Martin Van Buren, Vice President during the second Jackson administration, was one of the savviest politicians of his day and the logical presidential choice of the Democratic Party in 1836. His election received an assist when the anti-Jacksonians, who had only begun to coalesce into the new Whig Party, failed to agree on a single presidential candidate. Instead, three regional candidates—William Henry Harrison of Ohio, Hugh White of Tennessee, and Daniel Webster of Massachusetts—all ran. Hopes that their combined candidacies might draw enough votes from Van Buren to deny him a majority in the Electoral College, thereby throwing the decision into the House of Representatives where anti-Jackson forces held sway, proved futile. Van Buren won handily and continued the policies of his predecessor.

Campaign Results

Election Year	Candidate	Office	Party	Electoral Vote	Popular Vote
1836	Martin Van Buren	P	Democratic	170	764,716
	Richard M. Johnson	VP			
	William Henry Harrison	P	Whig	73	550,816
	Francis Granger	VP			
	Hugh L. White		Whig	26	146,107
	Daniel Webster		Whig	14	41,201
	Willie P. Mangum		Independent	11	--

Log Cabin Hard Cider Campaign of 1840

The White House contest of 1840, pitting incumbent Democrat Martin Van Buren against the Whig Party's William Henry Harrison, was one of the most memorable campaigns of the nineteenth century. Using the log cabin and barrel of hard cider as symbols of their cause, the Whigs sold Harrison to voters as a simple, rustic yeoman farmer not unlike many of them. Melded with this homespun imagery were frequent reminders of Harrison's early fame as a frontier soldier. Between allusions to his battlefield heroics and his taste for the simple life, his supporters generated a groundswell for his candidacy that the opposition was hard-pressed to combat. Among the most noteworthy aspects of the campaign were the massive demonstrations featuring an avalanche of log-cabin emblazoned banners, ribbons, and sheet music organized on Harrison's behalf. Never before had the country witnessed such a spirited political campaign. Generally missing from the Whigs' efforts was any discussion of issues, but the voters did not notice and Harrison claimed the White House with relative ease.

An 1840 Log Cabin

In making the log cabin and barrel of hard cider the symbols of Harrison's White House campaign, his supporters fostered an illusion that their candidate was pretty much like any rank-and-file voter. Nothing was farther from the truth. Born into an aristocratic Virginia family, Harrison occupied a spacious residence in Ohio and presided over a farm that far exceeded the landholdings of the nation's more typical farmers.

This log cabin was carried in a pro-Harrison demonstration in Lancaster, Pennsylvania, in the fall of 1840 and was again used in the presidential campaign of 1888 to promote the White House candidacy of Harrison's grandson, Benjamin.

Abraham Lincoln Presidential Library and Museum

Tippecanoe (and Tyler, too!)

To show their loyalty to Harrison, voters could chose from a vast array of pins emblazoned with the omnipresent log cabin. Or they could take their pick from more than twenty styles of bandannas and two hundred types of ribbons. Also available to them were such campaign novelties as Tippecanoe shaving soap and Tippecanoe tobacco, which took their name from the Battle of Tippecanoe in 1811 where Harrison had subdued a force of Indians. Voters could also show their allegiance by sipping whiskey from a bottle made in the shape of a log cabin. John Tyler, Harrison's running mate, inspired no similar degree of excitement.

Broadside announcing a pro-Harrison gathering in Alton, Illinois

Abraham Lincoln Presidential Library and Museum

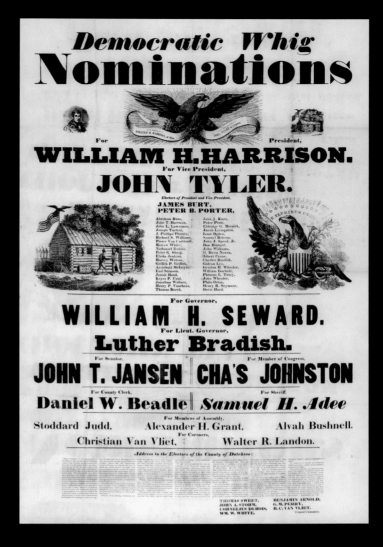

Ribbon from Harrison's log cabin campaign

Although Harrison was in his late sixties when he ran for president in 1840, many of his campaign items showed him to be much younger. The image on this ribbon dates back to his days as a frontier soldier at the time of the War of 1812.

Campaign Results

Election Year	Candidate	Office	Party	Electoral Vote	Popular Vote
1840	William Henry Harrison	P	Whig	234	1,274,624
	John Tyler	VP			
	Martin Van Buren	P	Democratic	60	1,127,781
	Choice left to state electors	VP			
	James Birney		Liberty	7069	--

1844
America's First Dark Horse

The Democratic nomination of a relatively unknown Tennessee Congressman, James K. Polk, as its presidential candidate in 1844 marked the first time that a major party placed its White House hopes on a "dark horse" candidate. In the wake of the unexpected nomination, the Whig opposition mockingly posed the question, "Who is James K. Polk?" and confidently anticipated what they now considered the all but certain presidential election of their own widely known and much beloved Henry Clay. While Polk could not match Clay's high national profile, he proved a formidable opponent. On Election Day, the Whigs' sneering question rang hollow as the Democrats' "dark horse" standard bearer claimed victory.

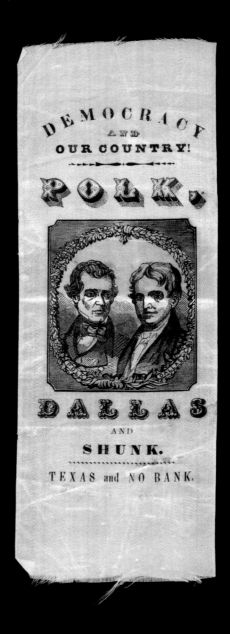

Clay and Frelinghuysen

The 1844 election was the last best chance for Henry Clay to realize his hopes for the White House, which he had nurtured since the 1820s. When he lost, this normally resilient politician succumbed for the first time in his long public career to a prolonged depression. Many of Clay's followers were also fiercely disappointed, and many of his supporters wept openly at the news of his defeat. "It was as if the first born of every family," noted one Whig insider, "had been stricken down."

Polk and Dallas

In 1844, both Whigs and Democrats took their cues from the lively log cabin campaign for William Henry Harrison. The candidacies of both James Polk and Henry Clay spawned a circus-like atmosphere across the country. According to one observer, "all the . . . paraphernalia of electioneering warfare are in active requisition," and banners announcing fealty to one or the other candidate were visible everywhere.

One of the handsomest of these banners surviving today is this meticulously embroidered silk standard made to promote the White House chances of James K. Polk.

1844	James K. Polk	P	Democratic	170	1,338,464
	George M. Dallas	VP			
	Henry Clay	P	Whig	105	1,300,097
	Theodore Frelinghuysen	VP			
	James G. Birney		Liberty	--	62,300

1848

The Hero of the Mexican War

By the late 1840s, a candidate's military distinction was a well-proven asset in presidential elections. But its full value did not become apparent until 1848, when the Whigs fielded Zachary Taylor as their White House candidate. Unlike past war-hero presidential hopefuls such as Andrew Jackson, Taylor could claim no political experience whatsoever. His sole recommendation for civilian office was his fame as the victorious general in the recent war with Mexico. But that was recommendation enough for most voters, and to counter the popular groundswell for Taylor, supporters of his Democratic opponent Lewis Cass produced images that sought to remind voters that in his younger days Cass too had worn the insignia of a general. The ploy of pitting general against general, however, was not enough to keep Taylor from winning.

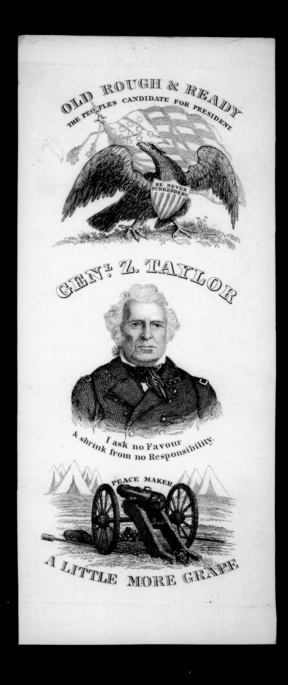

THE UNION IT MUST BE PRESERVED

☆

Democratic Ticket.

FOR PRESIDENT,

LEWIS CASS,

OF MICHIGAN.

—

FOR VICE PRESIDENT,

WILLIAM O. BUTLER,

OF KENTUCKY.

—

Electors of President and Vice President.

SAMUEL STARKWEATHER, of Cuyahoga
LEGRAND BYINGTON, of Pike
JOHN SNIDER, of Hamilton
GEORGE KESLING, of Warren
JONATHAN KENNEY, of Montgomery
G. VOLNEY DORSEY, of Miami
CHARLES M. GODFREY, of Putnam
SAMUEL MYERS, of Crawford
JOHN W. BELL, of Highland
DANIEL COCKERILL, of Adams
SAMUEL DIFFENDERFER, of Pickaway
STEPHEN M. LITTELL, of Delaware
DANIEL J SWINNEY, of Richland
LEWIS ANDERSON, of Lawrence
JOHN LIDEY, of Perry
WILLIAM LAWRENCE, of Guernsey
WILLIAM I FRY, of Harrison
JOSEPH BURNS. of Coshocton
WILLIAM McDONALD, of Jefferson
DAVID A STARKWEATHER, of Stark
JOEL B BUTTLES, of Trumbull
HENRY B PAYNE, of Cuyahoga
ABIJAH IVES, of Huron

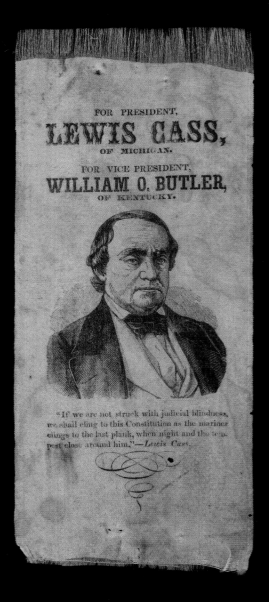

FOR PRESIDENT,

LEWIS CASS,

OF MICHIGAN.

FOR VICE PRESIDENT,

WILLIAM O. BUTLER,

OF KENTUCKY.

"If we are not struck with judicial blindness,
we shall cling to this Constitution as the mariner
clings to the last plank, when night and the tempest close around him."—*Lewis Cass.*

LEWIS CASS.

Wm O. BUTLER.

Campaign Results

Election Year	Candidate	Office	Party	Electoral Vote	Popular Vote
1848	Zachary Taylor	P	Whig	163	1,360,967
	Millard Fillmore	VP			
	Lewis Cass	P	Democratic	127	1,222,342
	William O. Butler	VP			
	Martin Van Buren		Free Soil	--	291,263

1852
An Able Soldier Rejected

The election of 1852 marks one of the few times that a military hero failed in his quest for the White House. Emboldened by the earlier successes of William Henry Harrison and Zachary Taylor, the Whigs chose General Winfield Scott, arguably the most capable military leader of his day. In the process, the Whigs passed over such party luminaries as Daniel Webster, referred to by his admirers as "Godike Daniel." Scott's opponent was Franklin Pierce, a little-known Senator from New Hampshire who had also fought in the Mexican War and had attained the rank of brigadier-general. The campaign, marked by partisan bickering about the military prowess of both "Old Fuss and Feathers" (Scott) and "The Fainting General" (Pierce), resulted in a victory for Pierce.

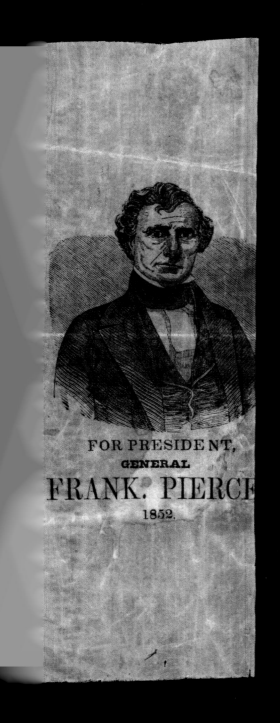

FOR PRESIDENT,
GENERAL
FRANK. PIERCE
1852.

Winfield Scott

W. A. Graham

Campaign Results

Election Year	Candidate	Office	Party	Electoral Vote	Popular Vote
1852	Franklin Pierce	P	Democratic	254	1,601,117
	William R. King	VP			
	Winfield Scott	P	Whig	42	1,385,453
	William A. Graham	VP			
	John P. Hale		Free-Soil	--	155,825

1856
A New Party Appears

As the long-standing debate over slavery approached fever pitch in the early 1850s, the two-party alignment of Whigs and Democrats began disintegrating. Out of the chaos emerged the Republican Party. Dedicated to stopping the spread of slavery, the Republicans selected western explorer John C. Fremont to be their first presidential standard bearer in 1856. Fremont's fame as the great "Path Finder" numbered among his chief vote-getting assets, but his surname also proved valuable as his Republican supporters undertook selling their stance on slavery to voters with the cries of "Free Men" and "Free Soil." After all, what went better with those two phrases than Fremont?

As this broadside illustrates, the Democrats were quick to counter with their own alliterative phrases. This broadside lampooning the Republican cause of 1856 cast Fremont as a champion of "Free Love" and a divisive promoter of "Free Fight."

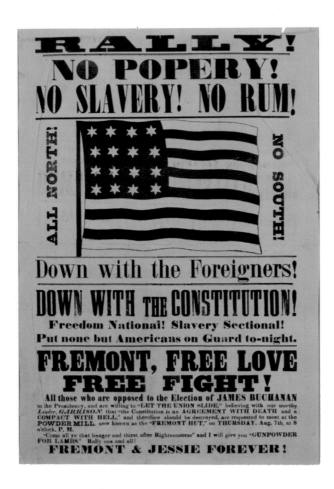

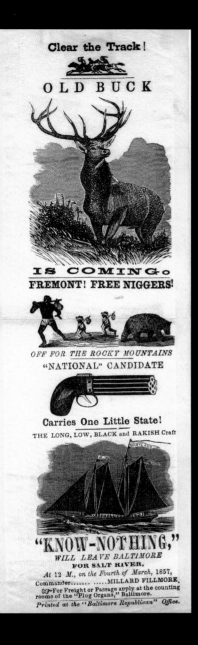

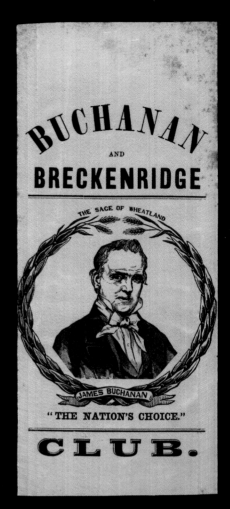

Ribbons from 1856 promoting the candidacies of Republican John C. Fremont and Democrat James Buchanan

Campaign ribbons document some of the basic strategies that the backers of John C. Fremont and James Buchanan took in handling the highly charged slavery issue in 1856. With its declaration that "The Union Shall Be Preserved," the Fremont ribbon sought to allay widespread fears that if he gained the White House, his anti-slavery position would force a breakup of the nation along sectional lines. Meanwhile, the ribbon for James Buchanan, hailing him as "Old Buck," played on the widely shared anxiety among white Americans that a Fremont victory would result in their being overrun by newly freed slaves.

The American Party Candidate

Drawing much of its strength from the anti-foreign, anti-Catholic Know-Nothing movement, the American Party came into being in 1854 and two years later chose former president Millard Fillmore as its White House standard bearer. Campaigning on a platform that sought to ease sectional tensions by curtailing slavery's extension while guaranteeing its continuance where it already existed, Fillmore's followers claimed that he represented the nation's best hope for peacefully resolving this intractable issue. In a contest in which Democrat James Buchanan ultimately emerged the victor, however, Fillmore managed to win only one state.

Campaign Results

Election Year	Candidate	Office	Party	Electoral Vote	Popular Vote
1856	James Buchanan	P	Democratic	174	1,832,955
	John C. Breckinridge	VP			
	John C. Fremont	P	Republican	114	1,339,932
	W.F. Johnston	VP			
	Millard Fillmore		American (Know-Nothing)	8	871,731

STRIKING THE POSE

ON THE CAMPAIGN TRAIL

Frederick Voss

Among observers of recent

PRESIDENTIAL ELECTIONS, THERE IS A WIDESPREAD CONSENSUS THAT THE MOLDING OF CANDIDATES' IMAGES IN WAYS CALCULATED TO WIN VOTERS' HEARTS HAS BECOME THE OVERRIDING CONCERN AMONG CAMPAIGN MANAGERS. IN THIS AGE OF SOUND BITES AND TV SPOT ADS, THIS HAS MEANT GIVING EVER SHORTER SHRIFT TO ARTICULATING ISSUES IN FAVOR OF CREATING QUICK, SUPERFICIAL IMPRESSIONS THAT ARE "PRESIDENTIAL" OR "COMPASSIONATELY CARING" OR WHATEVER OTHER QUALITY PROMISES TO STRIKE A POSITIVE CHORD WITH THE ELECTORATE.

To a large extent, the modern-day preoccupation with form over substance had its origin in Richard Nixon's successful White House campaign of 1968. When Nixon lost his first presidential bid in 1960 to John F. Kennedy, it was widely accepted that one of the causes for his defeat had been his first televised debate with Kennedy. By most estimates, Nixon had acquitted himself quite well in addressing actual issues. But when it came to visual impact, his pale, jowly, uptight appearance had been no match for the vibrant confidence that Kennedy exuded, and there is little doubt that Kennedy's overwhelming edge on that score became a factor in Nixon's ultimate defeat at the polls.

With that memory of cause and effect etched firmly in his mind, Nixon approached his 1968 presidential candidacy determined not to become involved in discussing issues. Instead, he and his campaign strategists concentrated on projecting a positive image to the exclusion of almost everything else, and their energies throughout the campaign were directed toward creating tightly controlled campaign situations, ads, and photo opportunities guaranteed to show Nixon off at his most appealing. Nothing was left to chance, and while his public appearances were made to look relaxed and even spontaneous, they were in fact minutely calculated to hide Nixon's often cold, stiff, and unendearingly brusque ways beneath a mask of engaging warmth, poised confidence, and non-specific statesmanlike rhetoric (fig. 1). The Democrats' White House hopeful, Vice-President Hubert Humphrey, found himself frustrated by this smooth veneer, and at a rally in Kentucky he sneeringly described his opponent as "that cool, that confident, that composed and that smiling Mr. Nixon . . . who campaigns without running, the man . . . who never makes mistakes . . . [and] either evades or straddles every major issue."[1] On yet another occasion, he declared Nixon to be no more than "an attractive package" all neatly done up by a host of "technicians . . . ghost writers . . . [and] pollsters."[2] But offensive as Humphrey found this situation, even he had to concede its effectiveness, and in the presidential contests following Nixon's 1968 victory, it became progressively clearer that the shaping of candidates into appealingly packaged images was becoming an almost all-consuming concern in White House electioneering.

While the slick packaging of Nixon in 1968 indeed marked a significant upswing in the emphasis on image-making in presidential campaigning, it was by no means the first time that such strategies had been enlisted to heighten a White House hopeful's allure among voters. The practice, in fact, dates back to Andrew Jackson's campaigns of 1824 and 1828, when his backers took every opportunity they could to remind voters of their candidate's glories as a frontier Indian fighter and, above all, as the general who had defeated the British at the Battle of New Orleans in the War of 1812. Doubtless even some of Jackson's supporters might have secretly

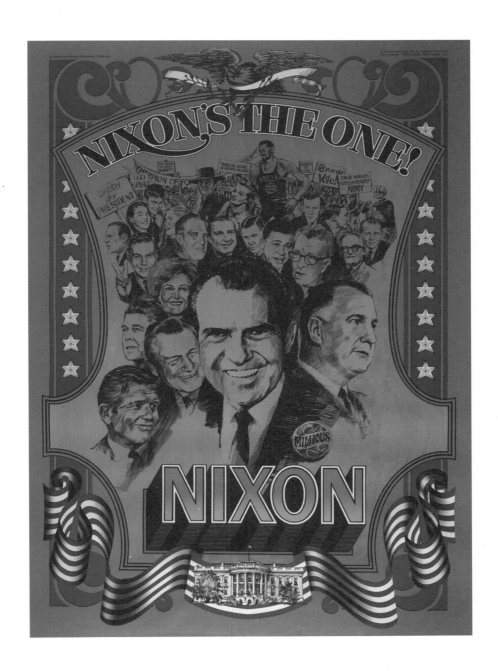

Richard Nixon Poster, 1968 (fig. 1)

The careful honing of Nixon's image in 1968 by his campaign managers introduced "presidential packaging" into the nation's political vocabulary. The phrase, in its several variants, received perhaps its biggest boost from Joe McGinniss's post-election analysis of the Nixon campaign, *The Selling of a President.*

Andrew Jackson, War Hero (fig. 2)

Andrew Jackson's supporters aggressively used his military record to promote his bids for the presidency. Widely disseminated images such as this one reminded voters of his prowess at the Battle of New Orleans and in the frontier Indian wars.

agreed with the contention, sometimes heard among his opponents, that military prowess did not necessarily make someone worthy of the nation's highest office. But the fact was that Jackson's military reputation invested him with an heroic aura that many voters found hard to resist, and ungermane though that reputation might have been to his fitness for the presidency, the Jacksonians were going to exploit it. Although Jackson had been long out of uniform, the campaign tokens produced on his behalf carried images of him turned out in military dress with captions meant to remind voters that he was the Hero of New Orleans (fig. 2). The ploy was not enough to carry the day in his first White House bid in 1824, but in 1828, against incumbent John Quincy Adams, it worked like a charm. As Jackson's followers paraded through towns with hickory branches alluding to the battlefield toughness that had once earned him the nickname "Old Hickory," they shouted "John Quincy Adams who can write/and Andrew Jackson who can fight."[3] The message was clear: the voter could cast his lot with the effete, Harvard-educated Adams or the manly frontier warrior, and in the final tally soldierly brawn carried the day.

The political value of Jackson's military persona was not lost on his political foes, and as his opponents began coalescing into the Whig party in the early 1830s, they too began thinking in terms of advancing their cause through personalities calculated to appeal to the popular imagination. Among the Whigs' first moves in that direction was their elevation of the anti-Jackson Tennessee Congressman Davy Crockett as a spokesman for their cause. The poorly educated Crockett never had much influence in Congress. But by the early 1830s, his great gift for weaving amusing and often exaggerated tales about his hunting exploits on the Tennessee frontier had won him a celebrity that would ultimately turn him into one of America's great backwoods legends. In the face of that celebrity the Whigs thus found in Crockett an ideal vehicle for promoting their concerns, and in 1834, the Tennessee woodsman embarked on a tour of the eastern seaboard to promote his party's cause.

But it was during the presidential election of 1840 that the Whigs finally hit their stride in the art of using public image to advance their interests. Their candidate that year, William Henry Harrison, was former governor of the Indiana Territory and a general in the War of 1812 who had served some brief, undistinguished stints in Congress. There was nothing in his past record to make much of a compelling case for electing him president. But in what was to become known as the "log cabin hard cider" campaign, the Whigs hit on a vote-winning formula. Combining Harrison's reputation as an Indian fighter with assertions that he was a plain, cider-sipping farmer living in a humble log cabin in Ohio, they transformed him into an amalgam of homespun simplicity and heroism that meshed exceptionally well with the country's egalitarian ethos (fig. 3). It did not matter that there was, in fact, nothing homespun about the aristocratically born Harrison, whose imposing Ohio residence stood on a farm of some two thousand acres. Nor did it matter that the Battle of Tippecanoe, one of the military exploits most highlighted in his presidential campaign, had been an easy victory over a relatively small, poorly armed band of Indians. What did matter was that Harrison's rustic image had great appeal for ordinary voters who enjoyed harboring an illusion that their future president was a hero drawn from their own ranks.

The ultimate proof of the effectiveness of this early exercise in candidate makeover was Harrison's election-day triumph, and in 1848 the Whigs set out to market their candidate, Zachary Taylor, in much the same way. A career army officer, Taylor was about as apolitical as one could be, and in fact had never even voted in a presidential election. But as the general who had just led American forces to victory in the War with Mexico, he had a charisma that made him eminently sturdy presidential timber. Better yet, Taylor's unprepossessing informality of manner and frequent inattention to the niceties of military spit and polish imbued this charisma with a common touch.

William Henry Harrison, 1840 *(fig. 3)*

As this ribbon testifies, the Whigs often melded their two favorite vote-getting ploys on behalf of Harrison—allusion to his military past and his allegedly simple log-cabin tastes—into a single visual package.

One of the most graphic evidences of how the Whigs capitalized on this hero's persona was a painting used to promote Taylor's White House candidacy. Commissioned by the proprietor of a Whig newspaper in Richmond, Virginia, it was the work of William Garl Brown. In it Brown showed Taylor in a post-war western encampment, informally mingling with members of his staff and dressed in the careless manner that clearly bespoke his disregard for the rules of military dress *(fig. 4)*. All in all, the picture was a perfect blend, reminding viewers of Taylor's military glories and, at the same time, portraying him in a down-to-earth manner to which average voters could relate.

Perhaps the most memorable nineteenth-century instance of image-shaping in pursuit of the presidency occurred in 1860. It all began in early May, at the Republican state convention in Decatur, Illinois, when John Hanks, the cousin of the mother of White House hopeful Abraham Lincoln, showed up bearing a pair of fence rails that he said Lincoln and his father had split some thirty years ago. Appended to the rails were flags and streamers and a sign reading "ABRAHAM LINCOLN/The Rail Candidate/FOR PRESIDENT IN 1860." The delegates loved it and called on a somewhat embarrassed Lincoln to verify the rails' provenance. The most he would allow, however, was that it was possible that he had indeed shaped these rails, adding good humoredly that "he had mauled many . . . better ones since he had grown to manhood." [4] Provisional though it was, that verification of origin was all his audience needed, and amidst roars of enthusiasm, the image of Abe Lincoln, the frontier rail-splitter, was born.

Following Lincoln's presidential nomination at the national convention in Chicago, the demand from Republican clubs for rough-hewn fence rails for use in public demonstrations exploded. Fence rails and the mauls and axes used to shape them quickly became the featured elements of border motifs on Lincoln sheet music and broadsides; the Republicans launched a campaign weekly dubbed *The Rail Splitter (fig. 5);* and images of Lincoln, his arms upraised in preparation for splitting a rail, became the focus of lantern slides and banners. It was, in short, a repeat of the packaging strategy adopted by the Whigs back in 1840. Only this time the vehicle for linking the candidate to rank-and-file voters was a fence rail instead of a log cabin. And like the log cabin before it, it too had no relevance whatsoever to the issues of the election.

Most efforts to clothe White House candidates in vote-getting personas have focused on trying to create images of homespun simplicity, soldierly strength, or masterful statesmanship. But in 1888, in promoting Grover Cleveland's presidential re-election, his supporters took quite a different tack. This time, the object was to invest Cleveland with bourgeois respectability, and among the campaign ephemera distributed on his behalf that year were a number of posters featuring images of Cleveland and the woman he had married two years into his first term, the beautiful, young Frances Folsom *(fig. 6)*.

This marked the first time that a candidate's spouse had been used in a White House campaign, and the impetus for this departure from electioneering norms lay in the campaign of 1884. In the course of that contest, it had been disclosed that the then-bachelor Cleveland had in his younger days admitted to fathering a child out of wedlock, and his Republican opposition had a field day using this breach of propriety to blacken Cleveland's reputation among the electorate. As a humor magazine of the day pictured Cleveland trying to hide from a sobbing mother and baby crying out for its father, crowds at GOP gatherings gleefully reminded the public of his wayward ways, chanting "Ma, Ma, where's my Pa?" *(fig. 7)* Ultimately, a youthful indiscretion was not enough to keep Cleveland from the presidency, and in the days following his triumph at the polls, Democrats were soon answering the Republican rallying cry with "Gone to the White House. Ha! Ha! Ha!" [5]

Zachary Taylor (center) with members of his staff at his Walnut Springs encampment (fig. 4)

This oil painting of Taylor by William G. Brown, suggesting his informal ways and easy manner with his men, became a centerpiece for an exhibition of Taylor images meant to promote his presidential candidacy of 1848. As with much of the Whigs' Harrison imagery of 1840, it served a twofold purpose, reminding viewers of Taylor's stature as a military hero and the often unassuming simplicity of his manner.

National Portrait Gallery, Smithsonian Institution

The Rail Splitter, *October 27, 1860 (fig. 5)*

Abraham Lincoln Presidential Library and Museum

Grover and Frances Cleveland, 1888: the picture of middle-class respectability (fig. 6)

But although Cleveland's indiscretion did not keep him from winning in 1884, his supporters worried that it might become a negative factor again in his rebid for the White House in 1888. To guard against that eventuality, they took the unprecedented step of producing promotional imagery clearly designed to remind voters that Cleveland was now a happily and eminently respectable married man. So it was that pictures of Frances Folsom Cleveland became an important visual element in her husband's campaign advertising, and instead of showing support for Cleveland by sporting the usual single lapel button emblazoned with the candidate's face, his backers were invited to wear a pair of buttons, one depicting Cleveland and the other his wife.

Among the best documented instances of consciously shaping an image in the quest for the presidency occurred in the late summer of 1924. Calvin Coolidge, who had succeeded to the White House on the death of President Warren Harding a year earlier and was now seeking to be elected to the office in his own right, was vacationing at his father's farm in Plymouth, Vermont. His reputation for being a man of few words had earned him the nickname "Silent Cal," and in keeping with that reputation he did not intend to make much in the way of public statements to promote his current presidential chances. "I don't recall," he candidly explained to the press, "any candidate for President that ever injured himself very much by not talking." [6]

But, if Silent Cal was not doing much talking on his own behalf, he understood the value of promoting his image and on August 22, he set off in a car to a nearby farm owned by his cousin to do just that, trailed by an entourage of reporters and photographers. Upon arriving, he took off his blue suit jacket, removed his tie and detachable white collar, and slipped into a pair of blue denim overalls. Grabbing a pitchfork, he was soon pitching dried grass into the back of a horse-drawn wagon. With ten Secret Service men looking on, three movie cameras and ten still photographers started recording the action as reporters took notes on how expertly Coolidge pitched the hay *(fig. 7)*. In seeking expert corroboration on that point, one reporter consulted with two farmers who had come to watch the spectacle. They told him that the President was indeed "an adept haymaker." [7] The point of the exercise, of course, was obvious. Here was a thoroughly premeditated case, if there ever was one, of attempting to sell a White House hopeful to the public by linking him to his humble past and all the honest virtues that that simple heritage supposedly bespoke.

As the pictures from this candidate photo op made their way into newspapers across the country, some observers expressed disgust. One opined that for "cultured Americans" at least, the sight of their President "pitching hay and milking bossy" was decidedly off-putting, and another complained that Americans were being asked to vote for Coolidge simply "because he knows his way around a barnyard." [8] *The New York Times,* on the other hand, was more amused than offended by this staged effort to identify Coolidge with New England rural virtue. He had pitched the hay, the paper waggishly noted, "without a suspicion of any joy of living" and in so doing, had invested this photo op with "the truest sort of realism." And for that Coolidge deserved congratulations, because performing his task with a "'joie de vivre,'" the *Times* declared, "would have been wholly out of keeping with a Vermont farm." [9] Perhaps more to the point, however, Coolidge should also have been congratulated on his shrewd intuition of how well this bit of vote-getting theater meshed with the romantic illusions that Americans harbored about their agrarian heritage.

President Coolidge posing for the press in the unlikely guise of a Vermont farmer in Auguest 1924 (fig. 7)

The Coolidge Collection, Forbes Library, Northampton, Massachusetts

Photo by Ron Sherman © Millennium Group 1976

Jimmy Carter, 1976 (fig. 8)

This poster showing White House hopeful Jimmy Carter alone in a field was clearly meant to foster an image of rugged, independent agrarian virtue.

So went the business of concocting vote-getting images on the path to the White House, long before Nixon's watershed campaign of 1968, when he and his advisers transformed it into a high art form. And so it has continued to go since Nixon: with a blue-jeaned Jimmy Carter striking an air of Washington outsider thoughtfulness in a Georgia farm field *(fig. 8)*; with a smiling Ronald Reagan, posed in a cowboy hat, that was meant to suggest a blend of warmth and tough-mindedness; with John Kerry, who never had much taste for field sports, seeking to curry favor with NRA-minded sportsmen by going hunting; with John Edwards seeking to make himself more photogenic by going for a four-hundred-dollar hairstyling; and with Hillary Clinton trying to draw a link between herself and a large portion of the electorate by repeatedly emphasizing her "middle-class" roots in the "middle of America." [10] It can only be hoped, however, that while candidate image-shaping remains a basic ingredient of the election process, voters will never lose their capacity to look beneath it to scrutinize presidential hopefuls for credentials of a more meaningful sort.

Endnotes

1 "that cool, that confident and . . . smiling . . ." in Albert Eisele, *Almost to the Presidency* (Blue Earth, MI: Piper Company, 1972), p. 371.

2 "attractive package" in Joe McGinniss, *The Selling of the President, 1968* (New York: Trident Press, 1969), book jacket summary of content.

3 "John Quincy Adams who can write . . . who can fight." in Lillian Miller et al., *'If Elected . . .': Unsuccessful Candidates for the Presidency, 1796-1968* (Washington, D.C.: Smithsonian Institution Press, 1972), p. 97.

4 "ABRAHAM LINCOLN/The rail . . ." and "he had mauled many . . ." in David Donald, *Abraham Lincoln* (New York: Simon & Schuster, 1995), p. 245.

5 "Ma, Ma! Where's my Pa!" "Gone to the White House! Ha! Ha! Ha!" in Lillian Miller et al., *'If Elected . . .'*, p. 248.

6 "I don't recall any candidate for President . . . ." in Donald McCoy, *Calvin Coolidge: The Quiet President* (New York: Macmillan Company, 1967), p. 255.

7 "an adept haymaker" in *New York Times,* August 23, 1924, p. 3.

8 "cultured Americans," "pitching hay and . . . ," "because he knows his way around . . ." in John L. Blair, "Coolidge the Image-Maker: The President and the Press, 1923-1929," *The New England Quarterly*, 46, no. 4 (December 1973), p. 521.

9 "without a suspicion . . . ," "joie de vivre," and "wholly out of keeping . . . ." in *New York Times*, August 26, 1924, p. 10.

10 "middle-class" and "middle of America" in *Washington Post,* June 2, 2007, p. 1.

The Rise of the Railsplitter

1860-1864

In the second half of the 1850s, one event after another contributed to an ever deepening national sense of crisis over slavery, and it was inevitable that the dissension on that issue would color the presidential election of 1860. Among its most visible effects was the emergence of no less than four White House hopefuls, all claiming to have peaceful resolutions to the slavery question. The divided Democrats split their support between Stephen Douglas and John C. Breckinridge, while remnants of the now dead Whig Party rallied to the standard of John Bell and adherents to the Republican cause stood behind Abraham Lincoln.

In the interest of broadening Lincoln's appeal to voters, the Republicans often temporized on their anti-slavery views during the campaign. Had he faced a single opponent in this contest, that strategy might not have proven valuable, but in this four-way contest, it doubtless helped to give him an edge, at least in the North. In the final count, Lincoln emerged the winner, having won less than forty percent of the vote.

A Four-Way Race

The ferrotype, a newly developed process for reproducing photographic images on cheap metal, added a new wrinkle to campaign memorabilia in 1860—a pin emblazoned with candidates' likenesses not that different from today's campaign lapel pins. Shown here are ferrotype images of all the White House candidates of 1860 and their running mates. Presidential candidates shown here from left to right on the top row are: Abraham Lincoln, Stephen Douglas, John Breckinridge, and John Bell. The vice presidential candidates from left to right on the bottom row are: Hannibal Hamlin, Herschel Johnson, Joseph Lane, and Edward Everett.

Campaign Ribbons

Campaign ribbons for Lincoln-Hamlin (left), Douglas-Johnson (top-left),
Bell-Everett (top-right), and Breckinridge-Lane (bottom)

Liberty

Fremont's defeat in 1856 taught Republicans that highlighting their anti-slavery position put off many voters, even in the North. They did not make that mistake in 1860. Instead of the phrases of "Free Men" and "Free Soil" used to promote their cause four years earlier, they generally confined acknowledgment of their anti-slavery position in their campaign paraphernalia to a more ambiguous call for "liberty."

Douglas on the campaign trail

Through most of the nineteenth century, it was considered entirely inappropriate for presidential candidates to take a visibly active part in their campaign for the presidency. Accordingly in 1860 Abraham Lincoln remained at his home in Springfield, aloof from the electioneering fray. But his opponent, Democrat Stephen Douglas, was not so reticent. By mid-summer Douglas was actively stumping the country on his own behalf. His departure from the time-honored tradition deeply offended many. *The New York Times,* for example, declared it "not a seemly or a welcome sight to see any man . . . fit for the Presidency . . . soliciting his own election."

In early October of 1860, after Republicans swept local and Congressional elections in the states of Ohio, Pennsylvania, and Indiana, Lincoln was an all but certain bet to win the upcoming four-way presidential election. Faced with that reality, his Democratic opponent Stephen Douglas shifted the focus of his campaign. Instead of promoting his own White House hopes, he began stumping the slaveholding South to convince its citizenry that despite the anti-slavery position of Lincoln's party, secession would be an unwise response to his presidential election. By then, however, the South's willingness to entertain this view was rapidly diminishing.

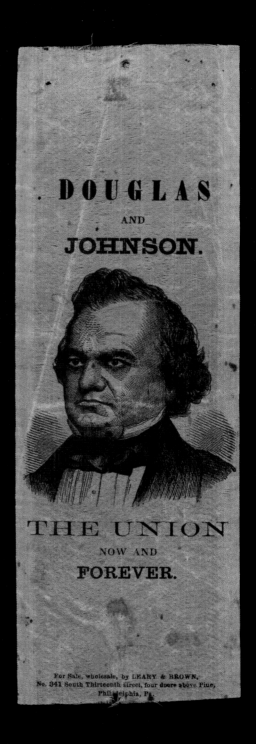

Campaign Plain Dealer and Popular Sovereignty Advocate, *October 6, 1860*

The partisan newspapers put out by Lincoln and Douglas supporters in 1860 featured spirited accounts of the forward progress of their candidates and the supposed setbacks of their opponents.

Abraham Lincoln Presidential Library and Museum

Wide-Awake Pictorial, *November 1860 (right)*

Among the most memorable aspects of the election of 1860 were the Wide-Awakes, groups composed mostly of young men whose specialty was colorful torch-lit demonstrations to promote Lincoln's candidacy. The first Wide-Awakes came together in Hartford, Connecticut, in early 1860 to support candidates in a local election. But following Lincoln's nomination, his supporters commandeered the concept, and by mid-summer there were Lincoln Wide-Awake clubs sprouting up all across the northern states.

Typically the Wide-Awake demonstrators carried torches and sported military hats and glazed capes. As crowds looked on, they sang pro-Lincoln tunes and marched in synchronized lines that often zigzagged in imitation of the split-rail fences that Lincoln was said to have erected in his youth. The ultimate proof of the Wide-Awakes' campaign value was the emergence of similar groups in support of Lincoln's competitors. But none matched the Wide-Awakes for color and enthusiasm.

Abraham Lincoln Presidential Library and Museum

Wide-Awake Pictorial.

FOR NOVEMBER, 1860.

HONEST OLD ABE MARCHING FORTH TO THE WHITE HOUSE.

A Lincoln banner used in a Wide-Awake parade

John Bell for the Union Party

As the candidate of the Constitutional Union Party, a coalition of former Whigs, John Bell sought to steer a course in 1860 between the anti- and pro-slavery forces that were rallying to Republican Abraham Lincoln and Southern Democrat John Breckinridge. But his voice of moderation satisfied very few. As one newspaper of the day put it, his middle-of-the-road temporizing made him "Nobody's man!" standing on "nobody's platform!!"

Campaign Results

Election Year	Candidate	Office	Party	Electoral Vote	Popular Vote
1860	Abraham Lincoln	P	Republican	180	1,865,593
	Hannibal Hamlin	VP			
	Stephen Douglas	P	Democratic	12	1,382,713
	Herschel V. Johnson	VP			
	John C. Breckinridge	P	Southern Democratic	72	848,356
	Joseph Lane	VP			
	John Bell	P	Constitutional Union	39	592,906
	Edward Everett	VP			

1864
An Election Amidst War

Abraham Lincoln's presidential re-election in 1864 was far from guaranteed, and even as late as Election Day itself, Lincoln was voicing concern over the contest's outcome, noting that "about this thing I am very far from being certain." Feeding that uncertainty were the rifts within his own Republican Party that three years of brutal war had bred, and it initially seemed quite possible that Lincoln's Democratic opponent, former Union General George McClellan, running with Ohio Congressman George Pendleton on a peace platform, might profit substantially from that infighting. Two Union victories, however—the fall of Atlanta to General William Sherman and General Philip Sheridan's successful campaign in the Shenandoah Valley—greatly improved the outlook for Lincoln, and in the light of his generous 400,000-vote edge in the final count, Lincoln's Election Day anxiety seems misplaced. Upon learning of his victory, he took special satisfaction in the fact that Union soldiers had given him more than 70% of their vote.

UNION FOREVER

FOR PRESIDENT,
Abraham Lincoln.

VICE PRESIDENT,

Andrew Johnson.

Peace Commissioners,

ULYSSES S. GRANT.
WM. T. SHERMAN,
PHILIP H. SHERIDAN.

LANCASTER
LOCOMOTIVE WORKS
DEMOCRATIC CLUB.

FOR PRESIDENT:

Geo. B. M'Clellan.

FOR VICE PRESIDENT:

Geo. H. Pendleton

WELCOME
TO THE
'HERO OF ANTIETAM'

GENL.

Geo. B. McClellan.

Thayer, Pr. 344 N. Second St.

Campaign Results

Election Year	Candidate	Office	Party	Electoral Vote	Popular Vote
1864	Abraham Lincoln	P	National Union	212	2,206,938
	Andrew Johnson	VP			
	George McClellan	P	Democratic	21	1,803,787
	George Pendleton	VP			

THEY RAN ANYWAY

THIRD PARTY CANDIDATES

Frederick Voss

Americans generally regard their

PRESIDENTIAL ELECTIONS AS COMPETITIONS BETWEEN CANDIDATES OF THE COUNTRY'S TWO MAJOR MAINSTREAM PARTIES. THAT PERCEPTION IS UNDERSTANDABLE FOR A NUMBER OF REASONS, BEGINNING WITH THE FACT THAT THE GREAT BULK OF AMERICAN VOTERS HAVE ALWAYS SEEMED TEMPERAMENTALLY AVERSE TO THROWING IN THEIR POLITICAL LOT WITH MORE EXTREME BRANDS OF POLITICAL ACTIVISM. YET ANOTHER FACTOR, AND PROBABLY THE MOST CRUCIAL ONE, THAT ENCOURAGES AMERICANS TO FOCUS IN ANY GIVEN ELECTION ON ONLY THE TWO MAIN PRESIDENTIAL ASPIRANTS IS THE ELECTORAL COLLEGE. GIVEN THE WINNER-TAKE-ALL PRINCIPLE THAT REGULATES ITS STATE-BY-STATE VOTE TALLYING, THE COLLEGE MAKES IT NEARLY IMPOSSIBLE FOR ANY BUT THE TWO FRONT-RUNNING CANDIDATES TO HAVE THE SLIGHTEST CHANCE OF ULTIMATELY CLAIMING THE WHITE HOUSE. IN SHORT, IT HAS LONG BEEN AN AXIOM IN PRESIDENTIAL ELECTIONEERING THAT A BALLOT CAST FOR A MINORITY OR THIRD PARTY CANDIDATE IS AN EXERCISE IN FUTILITY, AT LEAST IF ONE HARBORS ANY HOPE OF BEING ON THE WINNING SIDE.

However doomed to failure the candidacies of minority parties might be, presidential elections have rarely lacked third party entrants. Since 1900, the quadrennial roster of White House hopefuls has typically included the names of four, five, and six registered minority candidates, and in the elections of 1956 and 1960, their ranks swelled to more than a dozen. The causes championed by these aspirants have varied widely. For a good many of them it was some form of socialism. For others it was Christianity, world peace, currency reform, or reducing taxes. And for yet others, it was vegetarianism or prohibition.

The first bona fide third party movement to field a presidential hopeful was the Anti-Mason coalition that began taking shape in the late 1820s. The occasion for the rise of this faction was the mysterious disappearance in western New York of one William Morgan, who had penned an exposé disclosing the secret rituals of the Masons. It was widely rumored that in retribution for this betrayal, the Masons had murdered him, and it was not long before anti-Mason sentiment was giving rise to a political party intent on expelling Masons from public office. Among the Masons slated to be driven from office was the present White House incumbent, Andrew Jackson, and in September 1831, at the first nominating convention ever held by an American party, the Anti-Masons nominated the noted lawyer and former attorney-general, William Wirt, to take on Jackson in the election of 1832 (fig. 1). It was something of an odd choice, to say the least, for Wirt was himself a Mason, and he made it clear from the outset that he would not join in his party's attacks on Freemasonry. But his intense dislike for Jackson convinced him to accept the nomination anyway, in a hope that the country's as yet unorganized anti-Jackson factions would unite behind his standard. Having little taste for the hurly-burly of election politics, Wirt did not, however, lift a finger to promote his candidacy, and when Henry Clay later eclipsed him as the main anti-Jackson candidate of 1832, he remained in the contest only with great reluctance. When his defeat became official, America's first third party White House hopeful felt only relief. "A culprit pardoned at the gallows," he wrote a friend, "could not be more light-hearted." [1]

America's first third party candidate, William Wirt (fig. 1)

As America's first third party presidential hopeful, William Wirt was loath to alter his public image for the mere sake of pleasing voters. "I shall not change my manners," he said. "If the people choose to take me as I am—well. If not, they will only leave me where I have always preferred to be, enjoying the independence of private life."

National Portrait Gallery, Smithsonian Institution

In the two decades before the Civil War, the main impetus for the formation of minority parties was the ever mounting protest against slavery. There was a school of thought in the abolitionist movement that held that the Federal government's recognition of slavery made the government, by definition, so irredeemably corrupt that it was useless to try to rid the nation of slavery through the political process. But some abolitionists were not willing to close off that possibility, and in 1840 a newly formed political coalition known as the Liberty Party nominated James G. Birney as the nation's first anti-slavery presidential candidate. The Kentucky-born Birney managed to garner only 7069 votes out of the more than 2.4 million cast. But in the presidential elections that followed, abolitionist candidates did substantially better. Then, in the mid-1850s, as anti-slavery sentiment rose to fever pitch over the struggle with southern slaveholders for control of the Kansas territory, a dramatic shift in the political clout of anti-slavery forces occurred that can only be described as the fondest dream of all minority parties before and since.

In 1854, outraged by the inroads pro-slavery forces were making in Kansas, a group of anti-slavery activists met in a Wisconsin church to form a new political party dedicated to their cause. Thanks to the fragmentation over slavery of the nation's two majority parties, the Whigs and the Democrats, the new group did not spend much time as a minority faction working on the periphery. Soon known as the Republican Party, it drew anti-slavery Whigs and Democrats into its ranks by the thousands, and by the time it nominated John C. Fremont as its first presidential candidate in 1856, it was well on its way to assuming status as one of the country's two major parties (fig. 2). Four years later, with the victory of Lincoln, it was claiming the White House.

Following the Civil War, industrial growth and urbanization brought social and economic dislocations that gave rise to minority party presidential candidacies in ever more variegated abundance. But one of the first factions to field a White House hopeful was prompted not so much by changing conditions as by the sense of betrayal on the part of the now ascendant Republican Party. A good many of the converts to Republicanism before the Civil War had, along with being opposed to slavery, been prohibitionists who hoped that once slavery was eliminated, their newly adopted party would direct its reforming impulses against liquor consumption. After the war, however, Republican strategists balked at efforts to make prohibition one of its causes. In 1869, thoroughly disabused of any hope for promoting their dry crusade within Republican ranks, some 500 delegates gathered in Chicago to form the National Prohibitionist Party, and three years later, it was nominating its first candidate, James Black, for president.

The meager vote for Black, totaling 5608, did not bode well for the Prohibitionists' cause in national elections. Nor did the weak showings of their White House candidates in the next two elections. But, in 1884, the Prohibitionists set the wheels in motion for a marked change in the party's fortunes by giving the presidential nod to John P. St. John, the former governor of Kansas who had masterminded the successful campaign to ban liquor in his state (fig. 3). Although St. John knew he could not win the election, he was determined that his presence in the presidential campaign would "make the party a force that should be felt." Concentrating his party's campaign in a few crucial states, he was soon causing considerable anxiety among the managers of Republican hopeful James G. Blaine who feared—and probably rightly so—that the bulk of St. John's support was coming from individuals who would otherwise be voting for him. At one point these fears prompted an attempt to lure St. John out of the race with a bribe. But the "lion-hearted" St. John was not to be bought off, and although it will never be known for sure, it may well have been the votes for St. John in closely contested New York State that caused Blaine's loss to Democrat Grover Cleveland in the final tally. [2]

John C. Fremont in 1856 (fig. 2)

John C. Fremont's strong showing in the presidential campaign of 1856 transformed his Republican followers from a mere minority faction into a major political party, causing Republican optimism over its White House chances for 1860 to soar. "If months have well-nigh won the field," ran one post-election couplet, "What may not four years do?"

Prohibition Party hopeful John P. St. John (fig. 3)

The fact that John P. St. John's minority candidacy probably contributed to Republican James G. Blaine's defeat in the White House contest of 1884 stirred an urge for revenge even in his own state of Kansas, where he had once been much respected. Not long after the election results were in, the state's Republican legislature took out its anger by voting to rename the county that had been named for St. John.

Kansas State Historical Society

Certainly that was a commonly held view among Republicans at the time, and in the days following the election, party faithful in over one hundred towns burned his effigy. But St. John did not mind. He was too busy celebrating the fact that his perceived part in tipping the balance to Cleveland had made the prohibitionist cause a force to be taken seriously, and in the years immediately following, the country's two major parties, at least on the state level, became considerably more agreeable to taking more sympathetic stands on prohibition.

By the 1870s, the country had seen enough minority White House hopefuls come and go that they were more or less taken as a matter of political course. But when Victoria Woodhull announced her availability for the presidency in 1871, it was quite another matter. In an era that decreed a woman's only place to be in the home, the news was shocking, made all the more so by the fact that women did not even have the right to vote in federal elections. But the free-wheeling Woodhull was already well-accustomed to defying convention. Since arriving in New York in 1868, she and her sister, Tennessee Claflin, had worked their way into the favor of the aging railroad tycoon, Commodore Cornelius Vanderbilt, and with helpful advice from him, were soon the proprietors of a thriving brokerage house. Now known as the "Queens of Wall Street," she and sister Tennie moved on to found *Woodhull & Claflin's Weekly,* a publication dedicated to feminism and a host of other reforms.

Initially Woodhull was welcomed with open arms into the mainstream feminist movement. Her radical brand of feminism, however, went far beyond the movement's immediate focus on winning women the right to vote, and by late 1871, she was informing an audience at New York's Steinway Hall that she was a "free lover" and that she had not only the "right to love whom I may" but also the right "to change that love every day if I please!" [3] *(fig. 4)* With that, whatever claim Woodhull had to respectability disappeared.

Even so, she held steadfastly to her claim that she was still a White House candidate, and in May 1872 a motley assortment of fanatic reformers, styling themselves the Equal Rights Party, formally nominated her for president. Her campaign, however, did not get very far. In Massachusetts, the governor denied her the right to speak in Boston, comparing the prospect of her public appearance there to allowing "the undressed women of North Street on the stage." [4] Hampering her campaign further was Woodhull's preoccupation with disclosing in her weekly the details of two sex scandals, one featuring the philanderings of a Wall Street broker and the other, an extra-marital affair between the noted Congregational clergyman, Henry Ward Beecher, and one of his married parishioners. For exposing the wayward ways of these pillars of respectability Woodhull received little thanks. Instead, in the fall of 1872 she found herself facing charges of using the public mail to distribute obscenity, and on election day, the first woman to seek the nation's highest office was cooling her heels in a New York jail.

There is no evidence that Woodhull ever received any presidential votes. The first woman to achieve that distinction was Belva Ann Lockwood, who launched her first of two presidential campaigns in the summer of 1884. Lockwood unwittingly opened the way to her bid for the White House in a letter to fellow feminist Marietta Stow in which she observed that although a woman could not vote, there was nothing stopping her from seeking public office. Stow soon was acting on that thought, and in the summer of 1884 Lockwood learned that a group led by Stow known as the National Equal Rights Party had nominated her for president.

Compared with the colorful Woodhull, Lockwood seems decidedly tame and prim *(fig. 5)*. In her own way, however, she was every bit as ready as Woodhull to challenge the conventions of her day. Having experienced severe wage discrimination as a teacher, she mounted a lobbying campaign for a law guaranteeing equal pay for equal work in the federal government, and in 1872 Congress passed it. When denied entrance into law school,

"GET THEE BEHIND ME, (MRS.) SATAN!"—[SEE PAGE 143.]

WIFE (*with heavy burden*). "I'D RATHER TRAVEL THE HARDEST PATH OF MATRIMONY THAN FOLLOW YOUR FOOTSTEPS."

Harper's Weekly, *February 17, 1872 (fig. 4)*

One argument for voting for her in the presidential campaign of 1872, Victoria Woodhull once told an audience, was that having someone in the White House who shared her name with Britain's Queen Victoria would help to cement the Anglo-American amity. But as this cartoon commentary by Thomas Nast on Woodhull's unconventional views in such matters as free love suggests, a shared name may have been one of the few things that Woodhull had in common with this English monarch, who was known for her staid respectability.

Library of Congress

Equal Rights Party candidate Belva Ann Lockwood, 1884 (fig. 5)

Among the many witticisms inspired by Lockwood's presidential candidacy was the observation that she was the first White House hopeful "who never used a razor" but that it would be a mistake to "attribute this to youth." Another wag reported that Lockwood suddenly panicked when a crowd of supporters supposedly stood outside her window one night asking her to speak to them. "Oh, horrors! Save me!" she cried. "My hair is all up in curl-papers."

Library of Congress

Populist Party candidate James B. Weaver, 1892 (fig. 6)

Populist James Weaver's final vote count in the presidential contest of 1892 ranks among the most impressive in the annals of minority party White House candidacies. But having led the Populists to that peak, Weaver also led them to their precipitous decline four years later when he convinced his party to give up its separate political identity to back Democratic presidential hopeful William Jennings Bryan.

Library of Congress

she managed to go anyway as a privately tutored student. Then, when she set up law practice in Washington, D.C., only to find that her sex barred her from practicing before the Supreme Court, she lobbied Congress for a bill permitting women that privilege. Eventually she prevailed, and in 1879 she became the first woman allowed to argue cases before the nation's highest tribunal.

The news of Lockwood's candidacy in 1884 inspired a good deal of derisive humor. One newspaper, for example, announced that contrary to current campaign practices in some quarters, Lockwood did not intend to buy off the electorate ahead of time by dispensing rounds of drinks to voters. Instead, if she won she promised to reward supporters with a few sweets. "Bustle around girls," the paper thus advised, "and hoop things up if you want a caramel. Belva is going to fight it out on this crinoline if it takes all the rickrack in America." [5] But while her candidacy inspired wry allusions among the political wags to women's clothing, Lockwood took her candidacy seriously, and she made it the occasion for a lecture tour to promote women's rights. Still, she was not above having some fun with her presidential hopes, and on Election Day she quipped that, by her reckoning, she was the only one who stood a chance of defeating Democrat Grover Cleveland. The election, of course, did not come close to being the neck-and-neck affair between her and Cleveland that she predicted. When the votes were all in, the count stood at 4,149 for Lockwood and 4,874,996 for the victorious Cleveland.

Among the third party movements of the late nineteenth century, none had greater impact than the Populists. Drawing the bulk of its support from the country's agricultural regions, the party had evolved out of an increasingly bitter perception that the nation's farmers owed their ever recurring problems with heavy debt and falling crop prices to a rapacious oligarchy of bankers and industrialists. To correct this situation the Populists called for the inflationary monetization of silver. They sought a number of other reforms as well, including the eight-hour day, a graduated income tax, direct election of senators, and government ownership of railroads and utilities. In the election of 1892, held against a backdrop of deepening economic depression, the party's proposals for altering the status quo found considerable sympathy among the electorate. In the final tally, its presidential nominee, James B. Weaver, claimed more than a million popular votes and twenty-two electoral votes (fig. 6). Admittedly his numbers lagged well behind those of Republican Benjamin Harrison and victorious Democrat Grover Cleveland. Nevertheless, Weaver's showing was undeniably impressive. There is little doubt that it had a pivotal role in bringing much of the Populist agenda into the mainstream of American politics, which led, in turn, to enacting a good deal of it into law.

Among the most persistent of the minority White House candidates was Eugene V. Debs, organizer of the American Railway Union and a chief protagonist in the fiercely contested Pullman Strike of 1894. In 1897, he joined with others to found the Socialist party and in 1900 became its first presidential nominee. Debs understood well that many of his socialistic convictions were far too radical to win acceptance from the vast majority of Americans of his own day. But he harbored a hope that his presidential candidacy could at least begin to set the stage for a future more amenable to socialism. On the strength of that hope he ran for the presidency no fewer than five times.

Debs mounted his most memorable campaign in 1912, an election year when the cries for reforms in the nation's economic system were reaching a fevered pitch (fig. 7). Galvanized by those cries, he criss-crossed the country by train and for over two months kept up a schedule that required him to speak five and six times a day. One observer described his "raging" at the alleged failures of the two major parties to meet the country's real needs as "superbly spectacular," and in the end his efforts earned him some 900,000 votes—well more than double the number he had claimed in 1908. [6]

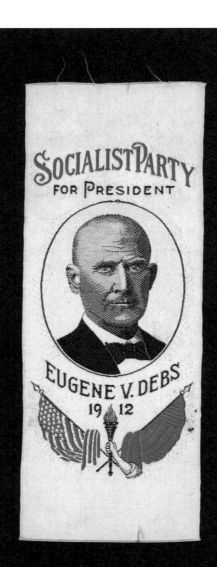

Socialist Party, 1912 (fig. 7)

Eugene Debs supplied the campaign of 1912 with a heated brand of rhetoric that doubtless struck fear into some mainstream voters. "Destroy all despotisms, topple all thrones," he urged. "Tear up privilege by the roots." But 1912 was a year when the tide for reform in business and finance was running high, and his often unmincing exhortations had considerable appeal among a good many of the electorate.

Eugene Debs, 1920 (fig. 8)

When he made the last of his five presidential bids from behind prison bars in 1920, Eugene Debs was pictured on many of his campaign buttons dressed in prisoner's garb and, in place of his name, was identified by his federal prison number.

No account of Debs's tries for the White House would be complete without mentioning his last candidacy. Sentenced to prison in 1918 for making speeches undermining the country's defense effort during World War I, Debs was still in jail when the election of 1920 came around. But that did not deter him from accepting his party's presidential nomination and from issuing weekly campaign statements that prison authorities limited to no more than 500 words. So it was that the American public had the chance to cast its presidential lot with federal prisoner 9653, and in the end nearly a million of them did (fig. 8).

Among Debs's presidential opponents four years earlier had been another third party hopeful, who unlike Debs and most other third party candidates did indeed have some real chance of winning. His name was Theodore Roosevelt, the country's exuberant twenty-sixth president, who had turned over the White House in 1909 to his hand-picked successor, William Howard Taft. Roosevelt, however, was disappointed in Taft's presidential performance and ultimately concluded that Taft had betrayed the progressive policies of his own administration. Never one to sit idly by in such situations, TR was soon competing with Taft for the Republican presidential nomination of 1912. As Taft quietly gathered support for renomination in closed party caucuses, Roosevelt was vocally creating a groundswell for his own GOP nomination in state primaries. Ultimately, despite strong convention support for Roosevelt, control of the convention's delegate-credential committee by Taft loyalists won Taft the Republican nomination. But Roosevelt's GOP backers, convinced that their candidate had been robbed of the nomination, could not accept this defeat, and after stomping out of the convention in disgust, they undertook to form a new Progressive Party with Roosevelt as its White House standard bearer. Self-righteously declaring "Thou Shalt Not Steal," Roosevelt accepted the honor with alacrity and after he likened his current state of health to that of a bull moose, it was not long before the bull moose was commandeered as both the nickname and symbol of his cause (fig. 9).[7]

Along with the catchy party nickname and logo, Roosevelt had several distinct assets that boded well for his candidacy. There was, for starters, the fact that he had already demonstrated himself to be an effective and quite popular president. Moreover, the times were in many respects ripe for the Progressive reforms he was advocating. In the final analysis, however, the splintering of GOP ranks that led up to his candidacy doubtless weakened the loyal voter base that would have been his had he won the Republican nomination. While the popular vote for Roosevelt exceeded by a good deal the count for Taft, it was not enough to defeat Democratic opponent Woodrow Wilson.

So the story of third party candidacies went and so it has gone through the twentieth century and into the twenty-first. On the whole, minority White House aspirants have continued to leave almost no imprint on the public memory and have had little impact on the country's political fortunes. Who but the trafficker in the most obscure facts in American election history would know, for example, that there was once something called the Texas Constitution party and that it fielded presidential candidates in 1956 and 1960, both of whom received recorded votes of over 15,000? And would the name of Henry B. Krajewski, 1952 presidential standard bearer of the Poor Man's Party, ring a bell with anyone? Or, closer to the present, how about the Constitution Party's hopeful of 2000, Howard Phillips? On the other hand, there continue to be from time to time third party candidacies like Prohibitionist John P. St. John back in 1884 and Populist James Weaver in 1892 that do indeed exercise a memorable impact on American politics.

Ralph Nader's Green party candidacy in 2000, for example, attracted nearly three million votes. Nader's effect on the outcome of that contest remains a highly debatable issue in some quarters, and the argument will perhaps

Progressive Party candidate Theodore Roosevelt, 1912 (fig. 9)

As Theodore Roosevelt made his way to dinner with his wife in Chicago just before the opening of the Republican convention in 1912, a reporter asked him about his health, and in response Roosevelt declared himself to be "feeling like a bull moose." The simile had great appeal, and when Roosevelt splintered off from the GOP shortly thereafter to become a third party presidential hopeful, his hastily formed coalition wasted no time in adopting the bull moose as its symbol of vigor.

never be settled beyond a shadow of a doubt. Nevertheless, a strong case can be made that most of the votes cast for him would, without his presence in the race, most likely have gone to Democrat Al Gore. Had they gone to Gore in closely contested Florida, the Democratic candidate, rather than George W. Bush, would have been the country's next president. Less speculative is the impact that the 1992 third party White House hopeful, Ross Perot, exercised on the American body politic *(fig. 10)*. With his reform agenda calling for such things as balanced budgets, Congressional term limits, and campaign finance reform, Perot claimed some nineteen percent of the popular vote—a percentage exceeded by only one other third party hopeful, Theodore Roosevelt. His appeal to voters did not go unnoticed among Republicans, who before long were commandeering much of his program to lure Perot's organized followers into their ranks. The recruiting campaign proved remarkably successful and paved the way for the Republicans' great victory in the Congressional elections of 1994, which for the first time since 1954 gave them control of the House of Representatives. Two political scientists, who spent several years scrutinizing the data, go so far as to suggest that Perot's campaign was not just one of several important factors bringing about that turn of events, it was the *sine qua non*.

Thus, hopeless as they may always be in ever reaching their most obvious and immediate objective, minority party presidential candidacies nevertheless have the potential to bear fruit. The fruit may take a while to ripen, and when it does, it may take forms that no pundit would have ever predicted. In a few instances, moreover, the fruit can prove as substantial as winning the presidency itself. And who knows? Maybe Belva Ann Lockwood is smiling down from presidential candidate heaven on the doings of the election of 2008 and congratulating herself that in some small way her try for the White House back in 1884 may have paved the way for making the gender of White House hopefuls into an increasingly insignificant issue. If she is, who would deny her that satisfaction?

Endnotes

1 "A culprit pardoned at the gallows . . ." in Lillian Miller et al., *'If Elected' . . .: Unsuccessful Candidates for the Presidency, 1796-1968* (Washington, D.C.: Smithsonian Institution Press, 1972), p. 105.

2 "make the party a force . . . ." and "lion-hearted" in Lillian Miller et al., *'If Elected . . .'*, p. 257.

3 "free lover," "right to love . . .," "to change . . ." in Mary Gabriel, *Notorious Victoria: The Life of Victoria Woodhull, Uncensored* (Chapel Hill, N.C.: Algonquin Books of Chapel Hill, 1998), p. 148.

4 "the undressed women of North Street" in Lillian Miller et al., *'If Elected . . .'*, p. 211.

5 "Bustle around girls . . ." in Julia Hull Winner, *Belva A. Lockwood* (Lockport, N.Y.: Niagara County Historical Society, 1969), p. 57.

6 "raging" and "superbly spectacular" in Lillian Miller et al., *'If Elected . . .'*, p. 334.

7 "Thou Shalt Not Steal" in James Chace, *1912* (New York: Simon & Schuster, 2004), p. 123.

Ross Perot, 1992 (fig. 10)

The Republican Hegemony 1868-1908

Six years after his party's founding, Republican Abraham Lincoln won the divisive four-way election of 1860. His and his successor Andrew Johnson's two terms established Republican control over the presidency that went virtually uninterrupted for the next half century. Until a four-way race brought Democrat Woodrow Wilson to the White House in 1912, only the election of Grover Cleveland to nonconsecutive terms in 1884 and 1892 interrupted Republican control of the executive branch of government.

Five of the six Republicans elected president during this 52-year period laid legitimate claim to military credentials established during the Civil War. And the sixth, the often bellicose Theodore Roosevelt, surely would have been able to make the same claim had he been more than a child during the conflict. All but McKinley served as general officers, although only the first of the postwar Republican presidents, Ulysses S. Grant, was a professional soldier. McKinley, the youngest of the five, enlisted and fought under Rutherford B. Hayes's command at Antietam.

Throughout this run of electoral success, the Republicans faced Democratic opponents whose claims to service during the Civil War were far less impressive. Horatio Seymour, Grant's opponent in 1868, served as New York governor during the war and, as a vocal critic of the Lincoln administration, took special exception to the Emancipation Proclamation. Grant's opponent four ears later, *New York Tribune* editor Horace Greeley, was at age 50 in 1861 too old for active military service: during the War he supported a Radical Republican agenda that was often critical of Lincoln's policies. After breaking with Grant, whom he had supported in 1868, Greeley found himself the surprise nominee of the Democratic Party in 1872.

Like Greeley, Samuel Tilden, the Democratic candidate in 1876, was too old for service as a soldier (48 in 1861). The only successful Democratic candidate for the White House, Grover Cleveland, hired a substitute, a perfectly legal if often criticized means of avoiding service during the Civil War. Of those Democrats who lost their runs for the White House, only Winfield Scott Hancock could boast of military service. With the exception of Ulysses Grant, Hancock was arguably the most accomplished military leader in the postwar generation to run for the nation's highest office. Hailed by the troops as "Hancock the Superb," he had played a major role at the Battle of Gettysburg. His loss by less than 10,000 popular votes to fellow Union veteran James Garfield in 1880 remains among the narrowest defeats in the history of presidential politics.

Attributing Republican successes during the latter half of the nineteenth century solely to the party candidates' stellar military records during the Civil War does the historical record a disservice. As the following pages illustrate, a broad range of economic and social issues were significant factors in many of the era's presidential contests. It is nonetheless undeniable that during this half-century many American voters rewarded Republican presidential candidates as members of the political party credited with saving the Union.

1868

General Grant
for the White House

Like Zachary Taylor, Ulysses Grant had no political experience to recommend him for the presidency. But as the most widely acclaimed Union general of the Civil War, he had a vote-getting potential that made his Republican presidential nomination and election victory in 1868 almost inevitable. He presided over an administration that soon gave birth to the term "Grantism," a shorthand summary of the public corruption and spoils abuses that characterized his first term.

Horatio Seymour, 1868

As governor of New York during the Civil War, Horatio Seymour had often been openly critical of Lincoln's war policies, a stance that left him vulnerable to attacks on his patriotism when he became the Democrats' White House choice in 1868. When measured against the stellar battlefield record of his Republican opponent Ulysses Grant, it was easy to tar him as a traitor. For many Grant loomed as the dedicated savior of the Union, while Seymour was depicted as its treacherous foe consorting with draft rioters and other foes of the Northern cause.

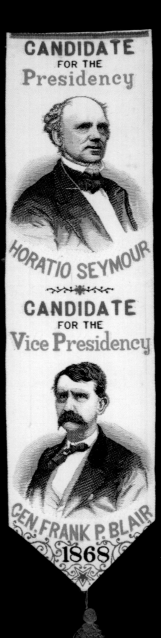

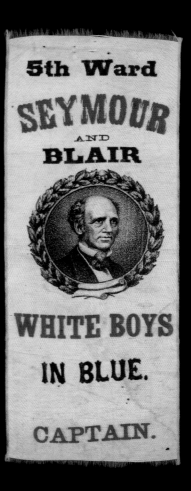

1872

The Sage
of Chappaqua Rebuffed

By the election of 1872, scandals had made "Grantism" synonymous with corruption. The Democrats and a splinter faction of anti-Grant Republicans chose the famed editor of the *New York Tribune,* Horace Greeley, to attempt to capitalize on Grant's shoddy performance. Eccentric in appearance, Greeley's affiliations with various reformist fads suggested to many that he was equally eccentric in his thinking, and he was subject to a series of wicked caricatures by pro-Grant cartoonist Thomas Nast. Grant, on the other hand, seemed invulnerable. Even evidences of wrongdoing by many of his presidential appointees did little to diminish Grant's own popularity, which rested in large part on his unassailable status as the savior of the Union during the Civil War. In 1872 he easily claimed the presidency once again.

The Candidate Caricatured

Greeley's bespectacled face, with its oddly wispy beard, lent him a slightly ludicrous aspect that made him an easy subject for caricature, especially when combined with the loosely hanging white coat and hat that he so often favored. No one was better at giving a ridiculous spin to these features than the pro-Grant cartoonist for *Harper's Weekly,* Thomas Nast, who produced this likeness for the English satiric magazine *Vanity Fair.* He also did one of Grant for the magazine that was not nearly so scathing. It is said that Nast's uncommonly harsh caricatures of Greeley during the campaign of 1872 were contributing factors that led to Greeley's severe demoralization following his defeat at the polls and perhaps even contributed to his death several weeks later.

Collection of Frederick Voss

MEMENTO OF CHAPPAQUA.

THE STAFF OF THIS FLAG

IS FROM THE

FARM OF HON. HORACE GREELEY,

AND FROM   BY THE

CHOPPINGS   PHILOSOPHER'S

AND

PRUNINGS   OWN HAND.

It is invaluable as a souvenir of our great Sage, Philosopher and Statesman.

"ONE TERM—ONE FLAG—ONE COUNTRY."

None genuine without these

CERTIFICATES.

Chappaqua, July 27th, 1872.

Mr. H. M. Graham has the sole authority to use the brushwood from my groves and farm at Chappaqua for Campaign Badges and Flagstaffs.

Signed, *Horace Greeley.*

The Chappaqua Flags, as issued by Graham & Co., are recommended by the National Committee of Liberal Republicans.

Signed, *Ethan Allen*

New York, July 22, 1872.   *Chairman.*

ORIGINAL CERTIFICATES ON FILE AT THIS OFFICE.

I hereby certify that the staff of this Flag is from the farm of Mr. Greeley, at Chappaqua.

H. A. Graham

The Flag may be attached to the clothing by a stitch at top and bottom of the Staff.

AMERICAN NEWS CO., Agents.

A Greeley Fund Raiser

The effort to raise funds for Greeley's campaign by selling little flags attached to "choppings" and "prunings" from Greeley's farm in Chappaqua, New York, doubtless found its inspiration in the Republicans' sale of pieces of fence rail allegedly hewn by Lincoln in 1860.

Campaign Results

Election Year	Candidate	Office	Party	Electoral Vote	Popular Vote
1868	Ulysses S. Grant	P	Republican	214	3,013,421
	Schuyler Colfax	VP			
	Horatio Seymour	P	Democratic	80	2,706,829
	Francis P. Blair, Jr.	VP			
1872	Ulysses S. Grant	P	Republican	286	3,596,745
	Henry Wilson	VP			
	Horace Greeley	P	Democratic	0	2,843,446
	Benjamin G. Brown	VP			

1876

The Stolen Election

Yours truly,
Samuel J. Tilden

TILDEN AND REFORM

Reduction of Taxation
—AND—
Honest Administration of the Government.

As Governor of New York, SAMUEL J.
TILDEN reduced taxation and expendi-
tures one-half; as President he will do
the same for the United States.
Tilden carried New York by 50,317, the
largest majority she ever gave
to any Democrat.

The deeply rooted corruption in the Republican administration of Ulysses Grant and a lingering economic depression led many observers to believe that the Democratic presidential hopeful in 1876, Samuel J. Tilden, was certain to break the Republican's sixteen-year hold on the White House. As returns came in on election night, a Democratic victory seemed assured. Both Tilden and his Republican opponent, Rutherford B. Hayes, went to bed thinking Tilden the winner. But the triumph quickly came undone in the face of allegations of voting irregularities in four states, and Congress eventually entrusted the investigation of these accusations to a special commission. After months of charges, countercharges, and backstairs bargaining, the commission finally declared Hayes the nation's next president. Who the rightful winner was in this dispute will never be known. The evidence strongly suggests, however, that Tilden may well have the dubious distinction of winning a presidential contest while losing the prize to which he was entitled.

CENTENNIAL ELECTION
1876

· THE DEMOCRATIC NOMINEES ·

Centennial Election, 1876

When the rancorous disputes over the alleged voting irregularities of 1876 were decided against him, Samuel Tilden believed that he had been wronged. Nevertheless, he accepted the result, declaring: "I can retire to private life with the consciousness that I shall receive from posterity the credit of having been elected to the highest position in the gift of the people without any of the cares and responsibilities of the office."

Tilden versus Hayes

Neither Samuel Tilden nor his opponent Rutherford Hayes had engaging personalities, and Tilden was an especially icy and aloof individual. But Tilden did have good organizational instincts, and his campaign was exceptionally well-orchestrated. Among its most effective aspects was a Speakers' Bureau that carefully instructed its speakers on how to adjust their pro-Tilden rhetoric to the interests and biases of any given audience.

A TRUCE—NOT A COMPROMISE, BUT A CHANCE FOR HIGH-TONED GENTLEMEN TO RETIRE GRACEFULLY FROM THEIR VERY CIVIL DECLARATIONS OF WAR.

"Tilden or Blood," Harper's Weekly, *February 17, 1877*

As the dispute over the election returns of 1876 dragged into the next year, Tilden supporters began to talk of resorting to arms if the commission investigating the voting irregularities denied him the presidency. To the rising cry of "Tilden or Blood!," Tilden counseled, "It will not do to fight. We have just emerged from one Civil War, and it will never do to engage in another. We can only arbitrate." But the fifteen-person commission deciding Tilden's presidential fate had eight Republicans and seven Democrats, and it was clear to many that peaceable arbitration was not going to carry the day for Tilden.

Library of Congress

Campaign Results

Election Year	Candidate	Office	Party	Electoral Vote	Popular Vote
1876	Rutherford B. Hayes	P	Republican	185	4,036,572
	William A. Wheeler	VP			
	Samuel J. Tilden	P	Democratic	184	4,284,020
	Thomas A. Hendricks	VP			
	Peter Cooper		Greenback	—	81,737

1880
A Boring Battle

The nearly issueless contest of 1880 between Republican James A. Garfield and Democrat Winfield Scott Hancock ranks among the least stirring presidential contests in American history. Even the charges of corruption against Garfield proved relatively minor and led to no great outbursts of indignation. As for the Democrats' Hancock, the most that could be said of him, one newspaper sardonically observed, was that he was "a good man weighing two-hundred and fifty pounds."

Election Year	Candidate	Office	Party	Electoral Vote	Popular Vote
1880	James A. Garfield	P	Republican	214	4,461,158
	Chester A. Arthur	VP			
	Winfield S. Hancock	P	Democratic	155	4,444,260
	William H. English	VP			
	James B. Weaver		Greenback-Labor	--	308,578
	John Bell		Prohibition	--	10,305

1884
Gone to the White House

The presidential race between Democrats' New York Governor Grover Cleveland and the Republicans' "Plumed Knight," James G. Blaine, sometimes seemed to be little more than a contest between catchy chants. Following a disclosure that Cleveland had fathered a child out of wedlock, the Republicans never tired of reminding voters of this moral lapse with their cry of "Ma! Ma! Where's my pa?" But Blaine, too, had skeletons in his closet, and in light of evidence indicating his involvement in Congressional bribery schemes, the Democrats were soon countering with their own cry of "Blaine! Blaine! James G. Blaine!/Continental liar from the State of Maine." Ultimately voters decided that they could forgive Cleveland's private indiscretion more easily than Blaine's public graft, and in the days following Cleveland's victory, the Democrats took to answering the Republicans' sneering campaign query with "Gone to the White House. Ha! Ha! Ha!"

Another voice for Cleveland.

Judge, *September 27, 1884*

This satiric commentary on the disclosure that bachelor Grover Cleveland had fathered an out-of-wedlock child implies that Cleveland hoped to evade acknowledging the truth of the story. But, in fact, once the tale was out, Cleveland did not hesitate to admit its accuracy, urging his supporters to "Just tell the truth." Such candor proved a good strategy. When compared with the evasions of his opponent James G. Blaine regarding his involvement in government corruption, Cleveland's honesty seemed all the more courageous and refreshing.

Library of Congress

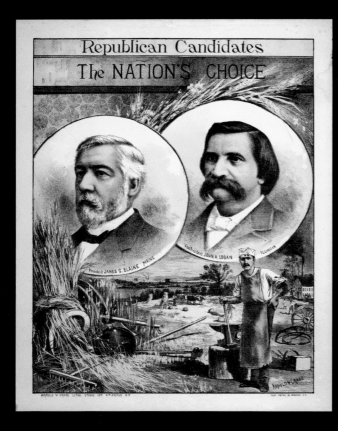

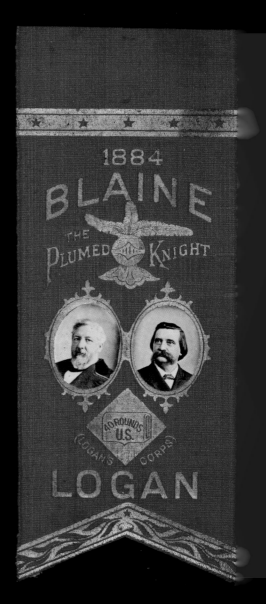

The Plumed Knight

James Blaine owed his defeat in 1884, in part at least, to his failure to disassociate himself from a three-word phrase used at a gathering in New York City where he was speaking. Before handing the platform over to Blaine, the Protestant clergyman charged with making introductions linked Blaine's White House cause to the struggle against "rum, Romanism, and rebellion." The words represented a slur on Catholics, most particularly Irish immigrant Catholics. But when Blaine got up to talk, he made no effort to distance himself from the sentiment, a failure that cost him a good many votes, especially in the key state of New York.

Third Party Candidates, Puck, *September 17, 1884*

The minority-party presidential candidacies of Benjamin Butler and Belva Ann Lockwood, pictured here as a carnival sideshow, added color to the election of 1884. The standard bearer of the Greenback Party, Ben Butler enjoyed considerable notoriety as the Union General nicknamed "Spoons Butler." A political opportunist par excellence, this one-time Republican hoped his Greenback candidacy would lead to a presidential nomination by the Democrats. As for Lockwood, her presidential nomination came from the newly formed Equal Rights Party. Although neither she nor any of her mostly feminine following were entitled to vote in 1884, she was not deterred from campaigning, and in the final tally claimed some 4,149 votes.

Library of Congress

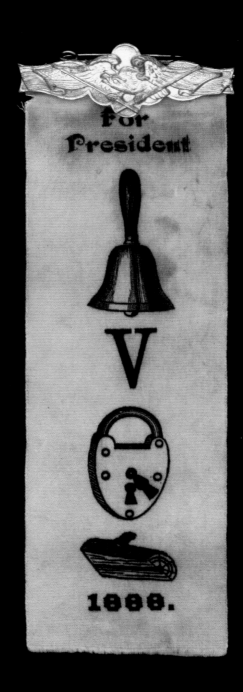

Ribbon spelling Belva Lockwood's name in rebus form from her second presidential bid in 1888

The Greenback Campaign, 1884

1884.
PEOPLE'S PARTY
FOR
PRESIDENT.
Benj. F. Butler.
VICE-PRESIDENT
A. M. West.

Although Butler had no chance of winning the White House on the Greenback ticket in 1884, it was widely thought that he might take enough votes from Democrat Grover Cleveland to give Republican James Blaine a victory. As a result, the Democrats tried to bribe him to drop his candidacy with promises of a position in Cleveland's administration. Butler refused, but did accept an offer from the Republicans, who wanted to keep him in the race for the same reason Democrats wanted him out. So it was that while attacked by both major-party candidates on the stump, Butler was secretly receiving much of his campaign funding from the Republicans.

Campaign Results

Election Year	Candidate	Office	Party	Electoral Vote	Popular Vote
1884	Grover Cleveland	P	Democratic	219	4,879,507
	Thomas A. Hendricks	VP			
	James G. Blaine	P	Republican	182	4,850,293
	John Logan	VP			
	Benjamin F. Butler		Greenback-Labor	--	175,370
	John P. St. John		Prohibition	--	150,369

1888

The Battle of the Bandannas

The White House contest between incumbent Democrat Grover Cleveland and Republican Benjamin Harrison has been called the Battle of the Bandannas. The inspiration for this textile war was Cleveland's running mate Allen G. Thurman, who routinely resorted to a large red handkerchief after taking one of his frequent pinches of snuff. To celebrate his selection as the Democrats' vice-presidential choice, convention delegates jubilantly waved their own red handkerchiefs. In the wake of that demonstration, the printed cotton bandanna soon became the rallying symbol of the Cleveland-Thurman cause. Before long the Republicans were countering with bandannas of their own, and evidence indicates that by Election Day, when Harrison claimed victory, Republicans had exceeded their opposition in bandanna consumption by some thirty percent.

Campaign bandannas of 1888 for Republican Benjamin Harrison and Democrat Grover Cleveland

Grover and Frances Cleveland

The story that Cleveland had once fathered a child out of wedlock had been used against him four years earlier. Doubtless the fact that he was then still a bachelor fostered suspicion in some quarters that he might be continuing on his wayward path. But by the campaign of 1888, Cleveland had married the beautiful Frances Folsom and in the process had acquired a new domestic respectability. To underscore his status as a family man and thus minimize the harm that dredging up the story of an illegitimate child could do to his second-term bid, his supporters introduced images of his wife into the campaign mix.

Campaign Results

Election Year	Candidate	Office	Party	Electoral Vote	Popular Vote
1888	Benjamin Harrison	P	Republican	233	5,447,129
	Levi P. Morton	VP			
	Grover Cleveland	P	Democratic	168	5,537,857
	Allen G. Thurman	VP			
	Clinton B. Fisk		Prohibition	--	--

1892

The Return of Grover the Good

Grover Cleveland's defeat of the Republican incumbent Benjamin Harrison in 1892 marked a return to the White House for Cleveland, the only president to serve two nonconsecutive terms. Economic discontent was the campaign's leading issue, and Cleveland's majority in the Electoral College was widely attributed to huge tariff increases pushed through by the Republican administration. The election also saw the first and most successful appearance of the People's or Populist Party in national politics. Its presidential standard bearer was James Weaver, who had first run for the presidency in 1880 on the Greenback ticket. This time around, he attracted over one million votes on a platform calling for the direct election of United States senators, the coinage of silver, federal oversight of the railroads, and restrictions on immigration.

Campaign Results

Election Year	Candidate	Office	Party	Electoral Vote	Popular Vote
1892	Grover Cleveland	P	Democratic	277	5,555,426
	Adlai E. Stevenson	VP			
	Benjamin Harrison	P	Republican	145	5,182,690
	Whitelaw Reid	VP			
	James B. Weaver		People's (Populist)	22	1,029,846
	John Bidwell		Prohibition	--	264,133
	Simon Wing		Socialist Labor	--	21,164

1896
A Cross of Gold

Against a backdrop of economic depression, William Jennings Bryan electrified the Democratic Convention in 1896 with his "Cross of Gold" speech calling for replacement of the nation's gold-backed monetary system with on based on both silver and gold. By the time he finished, he had made monetization of silver the central theme of the upcoming election and had made himself the hands-down favorite for the Democratic presidential nomination. In answer to Bryan's enthusiasm for silver, Republican White House hopeful William McKinley and his followers issued dire warnings that any departure from the present gold standard spelled universal ruin. The escalating heat of the debate made it difficult not to take sides. The contest between Bryan and McKinley took on an emotional urgency that by Election Day had turned the campaign into one of the most colorful in the annals of the presidency.

The Front Porch Candidate

Armed with funds totaling at least 3.5 million dollars, and perhaps a good deal more, William McKinley's 1896 campaign represented the costliest effort to date in presidential electioneering. Much of the money was spent on mountains of pamphlets, buttons, and billboard ads; not a penny of it went toward mounting a national speaking tour for the candidate. In keeping with the long-standing rule that presidential candidates should not seem too aggressive in seeking out voters, McKinley stayed home in Canton, Ohio, where his main occupation was standing on his front porch to say a few welcoming words to delegations of admirers brought there by train from across the country.

Ohio Historical Society

William Jennings Bryan

In contrast to McKinley's filled-to-overflowing coffers, funds for William Jennings Bryan's campaign were meager indeed. But armed with a gift for evangelical oratory, Bryan made the most of his slender financial resources. By Election Day he had traveled some 18,000 miles, stopped in 250 cities, and addressed audiences that collectively numbered in the many millions. Declaring that the fight for silver monetization boiled down to defending the common man against the country's rapacious bankers and industrialists, he spoke with an emotional fervor that impressed even some of the more doubtful. "By gum," said one man who had come fifty miles to hear a sampling of Bryan's now legendary eloquence, "if I wasn't a Republican I'd vote for you." Others were not so complimentary. Journalist William Allen White characterized his spellbinding appearances as the "incarnation of demagogy" and the "apotheosis of riot."

Bryan Bandanna

The voting public's intense emotional engagement in the election of 1896 spawned an unusual variety of campaign ephemera. The bandanna here was among the more conventional mementoes produced to promote the Bryan and McKinley candidacies. Depending on their political bent, voters in 1896 could bathe with McKinley or Bryan soap, walk down Main Street sporting a McKinley or Bryan cane, learn the hour by consulting a McKinley or Bryan clock, and savor their cigars using a McKinley or Bryan cigar holder.

Political Object Lessons

This novelty card, produced to promote the McKinley candidacy, offered voters an instant analysis of the dire consequences of putting William Jennings Bryan in the White House. Turn the wheel to reveal Bryan's picture and up pop vignettes of industrial unemployment and ruined farmers. Turn the wheel to show McKinley's face, however, and the card reveals pictures of humming prosperity on every front.

Gold and Silver Bugs

The battle over silver and gold in 1896 gave rise to a new pair of terms for classifying the country's electorate—the "silver bugs" and the "gold bugs"—and it was not long before makers of campaign novelties were translating the phrases into such insect-shaped novelties as the ones seen here.

Campaign Results

Election Year	Candidate	Office	Party	Electoral Vote	Popular Vote
1896	William McKinley	P	Republican	271	7,102,246
	Garret A. Hobart	VP			
	William J. Bryan	P	Democratic	176	6,492,559
	Arthur Sewall	VP			
	John M. Palmer		National Democratic	--	133,148
	Joshua Levering		Prohibition	--	132,007

1900

The Rise of the Rough Rider

William McKinley's vice-presidential running mate, Spanish-American War hero and current New York governor Theodore Roosevelt, was the liveliest aspect of the 1900 campaign. While McKinley himself took no direct part in the campaign, Roosevelt embarked on it with explosive gusto. With his fist-clenching manner, he was not just "runnin'," newspaper wit Finley Peter Dunne noted, he was "gallopin'."

The Full Dinner-Pail, 1900

With the depression of the 1890s fading rapidly into memory, the main slogan on buttons promoting the re-election of White House incumbent William McKinley was "the full dinner pail." Bryan and his fellow Democrats could not dispute the slogan's message that McKinley's first administration had witnessed a substantial surge in prosperity. Instead, they countered with a button declaring "No Dinner-Pail Lunch for Me!" and equating the election of Bryan with a veritable sit-down feast.

William Jennings Bryan, Anti-Imperialist

When William Jennings Bryan made his second run for the presidency in 1900, the call for silver monetization still was a significant part of his campaign rhetoric. But as this poster colorfully indicates, there were other issues that Bryan now considered equally pressing. Chief among these was the emergence of the United States as an imperialist nation with overseas territories following the recent Spanish-American War. At its best, Bryan said, imperialism amounted to civilizing other societies "with dynamite" and proselytizing them "with the sword," and he promised to take steps as president to rid the country of its newly acquired territories as quickly as possible.

Campaign Results

Election Year	Candidate	Office	Party	Electoral Vote	Popular Vote
1900	William McKinley	P	Republican	292	7,218,491
	Theodore Roosevelt	VP			
	William J. Bryan	P	Democratic	155	6,356,734
	Adlai E. Stevenson	VP			
	John C. Wooley		Prohibition	--	208,914
	Eugene V. Debs		Socialist	--	87,814

The Campaigns
of Eugene Debs, Socialist

In 1900, labor leader Eugene V. Debs made the first of four runs for the White House on the Socialist Party ticket. Although he always knew that he could not possibly win, he made surprisingly respectable showings in some of those bids and firmly believed that his repeated candidacies were creating a momentum for the eventual transformation of his country into a socialized democracy. That never happened, but there is little doubt that Debs's candidacies contributed substantially to the color of the early twentieth century's presidential electioneering.

The election of 1912 marked Debs's best-remembered presidential bid. As he traveled across the nation, the progressive reform movement was running at high tide, and a mounting sense that government curbs on big business were needed made the electorate more receptive than ever to Debs's call for a socialist order. Wherever he went, his audience was apt to number in the several thousands, and when he stepped out before a crowd of fifteen thousand at Madison Square Garden the cheering lasted some twenty-nine minutes. By the election of 1920, Debs was serving a prison term for publicly opposing the country's war effort during World War I, but he ran anyway.

An engaging amalgam of kindness, sincerity, and fervor, Debs was nearly irresistible on the campaign trail, and his cries to "destroy all despotisms [and] topple over all thrones" were apt to draw larger crowds than the speeches of his major-party opponents.

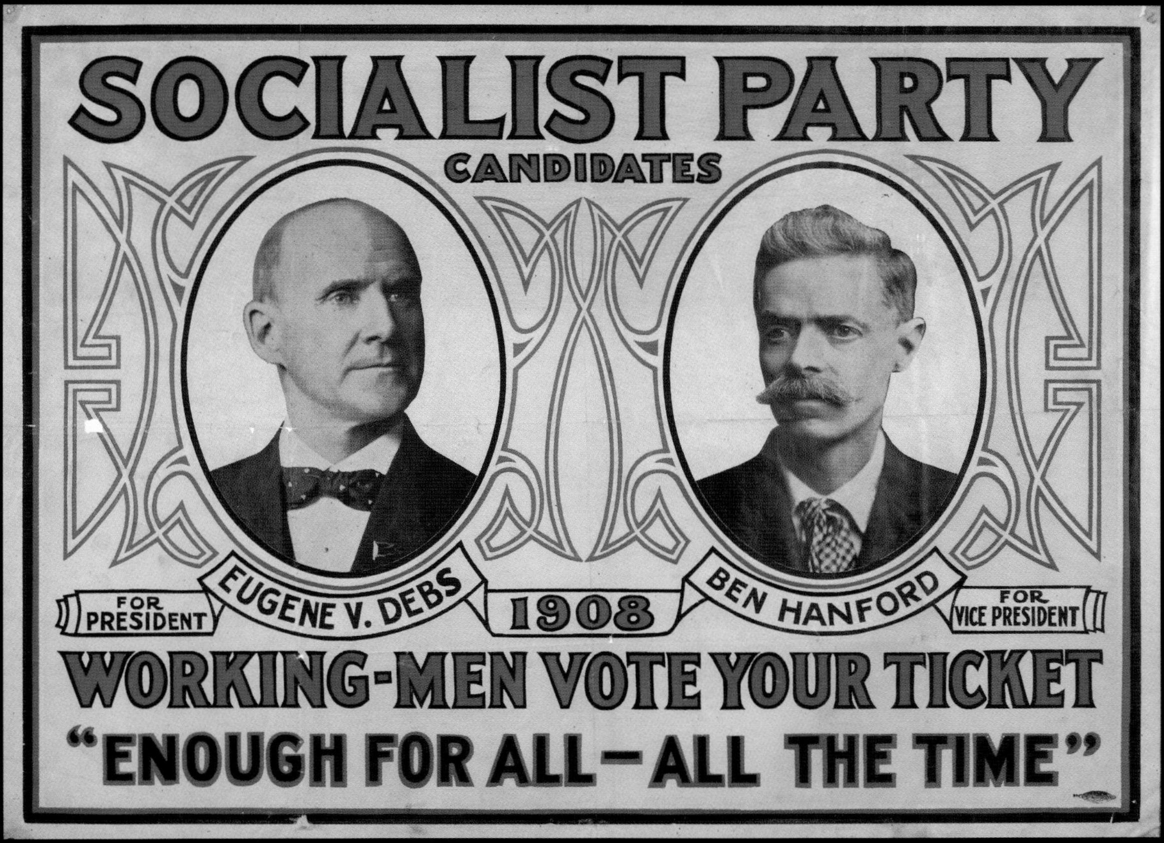
SOCIALIST PARTY
CANDIDATES
FOR PRESIDENT
EUGENE V. DEBS
1908
BEN HANFORD
FOR VICE PRESIDENT
WORKING-MEN VOTE YOUR TICKET
"ENOUGH FOR ALL—ALL THE TIME"

1904
A Landslide for
"That Damned Cowboy"

When William McKinley fell to an assassin's bullet in 1901, the ascension of Vice President Theodore Roosevelt to the White House caused grave concern among many establishment Republicans. Although TR had his zealous supporters, the attitude of many Republican leaders was epitomized by Mark Hanna, McKinley's mentor, who told his protégé upon his election in 1900 that "Your duty to the country is to live for the next four years from next March."

By 1904, however, "that damned cowboy," as Hanna dubbed the energetic president, had established an unassailable position within his party. His reformist zeal and obvious delight in the political arena made him an extremely appealing candidate. The Democrats did little to help their electoral chances when they nominated Alton Parker, an able but somewhat nondescript lawyer and judge from New York. In turning to Parker, the Democrats were rejecting many of the positions advocated by William Jennings Bryan during his campaigns in 1896 and 1900, most particularly his advocacy of bi-metallism. A return to support for the gold standard and other conservative postures did little for the Democratic cause. Roosevelt won 58% of the popular vote and swept all but the southern states.

Campaign Results

Election Year	Candidate	Office	Party	Electoral Vote	Popular Vote
1904	Theodore Roosevelt	P	Republican	336	7,628,461
	Charles W. Fairbanks	VP			
	Alton B. Parker	P	Democratic	140	5,084,223
	Henry G. Davis	VP			
	Eugene V. Debs		Socialist	--	402,283
	Silas C. Swallow		Prohibition	--	258,536
	Thomas E. Watson		People's	--	117,183

1908
A Successor for TR

After serving nearly two full terms as president, Teddy Roosevelt chose not to run in 1908. Sure that his progressive agenda would be in safe hands, he tapped his friend and Secretary of War, William Howard Taft, to succeed him as the Republican standard bearer. The Democrats turned for a third time to William Jennings Bryan. Although the Great Commoner sought to broaden his appeal to labor, he received his worst defeat in his three tries for the White House.

Campaign Results

Election Year	Candidate	Office	Party	Electoral Vote	Popular Vote
1908	William H. Taft	P	Republican	321	7,675,320
	James S. Sherman	VP			
	William J. Bryan	P	Democratic	162	6,412,294
	John W. Kern	VP			
	Eugene V. Debs		Socialist	--	420,793
	Eugene W. Chafin		Prohibition	--	253,840
	Thomas L. Hisgen		Independence	--	82,872

VITRIOL FOR VOTES

The Politics of the Slur and Smear

Rick Beard

By November 5, 2008, post-World

War II baby boomers will have lived through sixteen presidential campaigns, and most will remember some aspect of all but Harry Truman's 1948 upset victory. We will have variously praised or condemned five Democrats and six Republicans in the White House as well as endured one assassination and one resignation. We will have seen the strategies for wooing votes evolve from Harry Truman's whistle-stop campaign in 1948 through the primitive television ads of the early 1950s to today's seemingly endless debates and 24/7 cable news cycles. We will have witnessed Adlai Stevenson's "holey" shoe, Richard Nixon's maudlin "Checkers" speech, the first televised debates of John Kennedy and Richard Nixon, the riotous 1968 Democratic convention in Chicago, a tearful Edmund Muskie in New Hampshire, the Watergate break-in, the "capsized" campaign of Gary Hart, Michael Dukakis's embarrassing ride in a tank, Willie Horton, a "Swift-Boated" John Kerry, and countless other moments of high and low campaign drama.

Because Americans are easily persuaded that events of the moment are unprecedented, it is well to remember our ahistorical bent when considering presidential politics. While each campaign is to some degree different, for nearly two hundred years all have featured a combination of high-minded rhetoric and often vicious personal attacks. Few topics have been out of bounds when occupancy of the White House has been at stake. Sexual indiscretions, religious beliefs, military accomplishments, alleged and demonstrated instances of political corruption, and other topics, many with little bearing on the candidate's suitability to be chief executive, have all been grist for the political mill. A chronicle of the ways in which these and other topics have been put to use in presidential contests could fill multiple volumes. But in this instance, three particular elections – those of 1828, 1884, and 1928 – serve as instructive exemplars.

Old Hickory and the Adamsites

The presidential campaign of 1828 was a watershed in American political history. Although previous campaigns for a White House term had not been as sedate as is often portrayed—in 1800, for example, one opponent characterized Thomas Jefferson as a "howling atheist"—the 1828 contest featured an unprecedented level of personal attacks from both political camps as well as a flood of memorabilia designed to attract the attention of an expanding electorate.[1] The election was a grudge match, for Andrew Jackson and his followers believed (with some reason) that John Quincy Adams had stolen the election from them four years earlier by striking a "corrupt bargain" with Henry Clay, Speaker of the House (fig. 1). Although Jackson won a plurality of the popular votes cast in 1824, neither he nor any of his three opponents—Adams, Clay, or William Crawford of Georgia—won a majority of the electoral votes. When the House of Representatives was called on to elect a president from among the three top vote-getters, Clay, no longer in the running, threw his support to Adams, thus paving the way for the New Englander's ultimate victory.

Cigar Box, 1844 (fig. 1)

Henry Clay, one of nineteenth century's greatest political leaders, was an unsuccessful presidential candidate three times – in 1824, 1832, and 1844. During his long service as a U. S. Senator from Kentucky, he crafted both the Missouri Compromise of 1820 and the Compromise of 1850 in vain efforts to contain the heated and divisive debate over slavery's spread.

When Adams then returned the favor by making Clay his Secretary of State, Jackson's supporters were outraged. Convinced that Jackson had been cheated of the prize that was rightfully his by virtue of the popular vote, they swore to avenge this injustice in the next election.

Few elections in American history have featured such strikingly different campaigns as did the 1828 contest. Jackson, a self-made planter of the Tennessee frontier and the hero of the Battle of New Orleans, represented what Adams's supporters labeled the "howl of democracy."[2] *(fig. 2)* Son of the nation's second president, Adams was an erudite, well-traveled man whose background stood in stark contrast to the ruder credentials of his opponent. Determined that they would not lose the presidency a second time, Jackson supporters organized themselves into what would become the modern Democratic Party. They were disciplined and passionate, creating partisan newspapers, organizing political clubs to sponsor large public rallies, and persistently portraying the New Englander as an aristocratic spendthrift out of touch with the needs of the public. Adams's cold and often abrasive personality, which led one observer to describe him as "doggedly and systematically repulsive . . . with a vinegar aspect," no doubt did little to help his cause.[3] *(fig. 3)*

The election campaign had a bit of everything, but accusations of sexual indiscretion and military transgression led the way. One of the most unlikely charges centered around Adams's service as the United States' first minister to Russia, when, alleged Jackson's supporters, Adams had arranged an illicit liaison between Czar Alexander I and a young American woman. For good measure, Adams was also accused, albeit briefly, of having engaged in premarital sex with his wife, Louisa Catherine Johnson, whom he had courted and married while in London in the late 1790s. Adams supporters were not to be outdone. Rachel Jackson's failure to finalize her divorce from her first husband before marrying Jackson over thirty years earlier had long hung like a dark cloud over Jackson's political life, and Adams's supporters seized on this as proof of Jackson's unfitness for the presidential mansion. One bit of campaign doggerel emblazoned on a campaign banner – "The ABC of Democracy" – referred to "The Adulteress/The Bully/And the Cuckold" and epitomized the uninhibited character of the assault.[4] This exercise in personal defamation, however, took on a tragic poignancy when Rachel died in December 1828 after a long illness. Jackson believed the attacks had hastened her death, and he never forgave his opponents. "Those vile wretches who have slandered her must look to God for mercy," he raged. As for Henry Clay, who had helped engineer the smear, he was, wrote Jackson, "the basest, meanest scoundrel that ever disgraced the image of his God."[5]

Not surprisingly, the most persistent and telling attacks on Jackson dealt with his military exploits. Although Jackson's greatest triumph, his victory over British forces at the Battle of New Orleans, had occurred over ten years before his run for the presidency, the pro-Jackson medallions, engravings, and other campaign memorabilia more often than not portrayed him in military uniform. In response to these celebrations of military accomplishment, Adams's partisans countered with what was the single most memorable campaign smear to emerge from the 1828 election, the "Coffin Handbill," a densely printed bill of particulars charging Jackson with responsibility for the allegedly unjust executions in 1813 of six soldiers convicted of mutiny, as well as several other miscarriages of military justice *(fig. 4)*.

The attacks ultimately had little effect: Jackson won an easy victory, gaining 56% of the popular vote and 178 of a possible 261 electoral votes. But the election signaled significant changes, in both the American electorate and the way presidential candidates appealed to it. With the voter base greatly enlarged thanks to the elimination of property and tax-paying requirements, presidential campaigning was gravitating toward

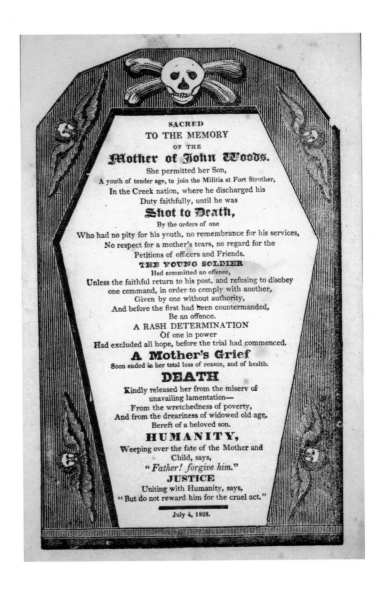

SACRED
TO THE MEMORY
OF THE
Mother of John Woods.
She permitted her Son,
A youth of tender age, to join the Militia at Fort Strother,
In the Creek nation, where he discharged his
Duty faithfully, until he was
Shot to Death,
By the orders of one
Who had no pity for his youth, no remembrance for his services,
No respect for a mother's tears, no regard for the
Petitions of officers and Friends.
THE YOUNG SOLDIER
Had committed no offence,
Unless the faithful return to his post, and refusing to disobey
one command, in order to comply with another,
Given by one without authority,
And before the first had been countermanded,
Be an offence.
A RASH DETERMINATION
Of one in power
Had excluded all hope, before the trial had commenced.
A Mother's Grief
Soon ended in her total loss of reason, and of health.
DEATH
Kindly released her from the misery of
unavailing lamentation—
From the wretchedness of poverty,
And from the dreariness of widowed old age,
Bereft of a beloved son.
HUMANITY,
Weeping over the fate of the Mother and
Child, says,
"Father! forgive him."
JUSTICE
Uniting with Humanity, says,
"But do not reward him for the cruel act."

July 4, 1828.

Campaign token for Andrew Jackson (top) (fig. 2)

Campaign token for John Quincy Adams (fig. 3)

One of several handbills issued in 1828 by Adams's supporters accusing Jackson of military crimes (fig. 4)

James G. Blaine, 1884 (top) (fig. 5)

Grover Cleveland, 1884 (fig. 6)

strategies that played to the collective emotions of the crowd. In the process, presidential politics became a far less genteel exercise, and the vitriol of smear and slander was becoming an ever more common element in the quadrennial presidential race.

THE PLUMED KNIGHT VERSUS GROVER THE GOOD

At the 1884 Republican convention in Chicago, the chaplain asked that "the coming political campaign may be conducted with that decency, intelligence, patriotism, and dignity of temper which becomes a free and intelligent people."[6] The ensuing electoral campaign between Democrat Grover Cleveland and Republican James G. Blaine suggests that no one was listening, for "dignity of temper" was notably absent from a presidential contest that is generally considered one of the dirtiest in American presidential history. Sex, religion, and political corruption all figured prominently in a close victory for the Democrats, who had been shut out of the White House since 1861. In the words of one noted historian, the campaign boiled down to a choice between a candidate who was "delinquent in office but blameless in private life" and one who was "a model of official integrity but culpable in his personal relations."[7]

Blaine, the "Plumed Knight" to his many followers, was the better known of the two candidates *(fig. 5)*. His long congressional tenure included the House speakership and a senatorial seat representing Maine; he also served as Secretary of State during the Garfield and Arthur administrations. Cleveland's more modest political career included service as Sheriff of Erie County, Mayor of Buffalo, and Governor of New York. His motto—"Public Office is a Public Trust"—combined with his reform-minded policies to earn him the sobriquet "Grover the Good" *(fig. 6)*. But both men proved to have pasts that would haunt them during the campaign.

Blaine, claimed E. L. Godkin, editor of *The Nation* and the *New York Evening Post,* "wallowed in spoils like a rhinoceros in an African pool."[8] An earlier try for the presidency, his attempt to win the Republican nomination in 1876, had foundered after a congressional committee investigating corruption got its hands on a series of letters the Maine politician had written documenting his profitable interactions with a railroad company seeking government favor. These so-called "Mulligan letters," named for the man who had revealed them at the congressional hearings, re-emerged as an issue in 1884 with the wide circulation of one of them in which Blaine had entreated its recipient to "Burn this letter." As the story of this malfeasance took on a new life, Blaine proved to be anything but a unifying force for his party. Longtime rival Roscoe Conkling, himself no stranger to political shenanigans, responded to a request that he endorse Blaine by noting, "Gentleman, you have been misinformed. I have given up criminal law."[9] Many other Republicans found the Blaine candidacy so distasteful that they broke away to create a loosely knit reform wing of the party labeled "Mugwumps," who included among their number the young New York assemblyman and future president Theodore Roosevelt.

Meanwhile, Grover Cleveland was having to deal with scandal of an entirely different sort. A bachelor when he ran for the presidency (he later became the first president to marry while in the White House), Cleveland had years earlier accepted paternity for a child born to a Buffalo widow named Maria Halpin. Although that admission may simply have been intended to protect one of his married friends who had also kept company with Mrs. Halpin, Cleveland had behaved honorably in the matter and accepted full financial responsibility for raising the child and providing ongoing financial support. Furthermore, when his secret was exposed, he urged his supporters to "Tell the Truth." Nonetheless, this bombshell gave Republicans a ready comeback to the Democratic chant of "Blaine, Blaine, James G. Blaine/the continental liar from the state of Maine"—they were soon rallying voters with the cry of: "Ma! Ma! Where's my Pa?"[10] *(fig. 7)*.

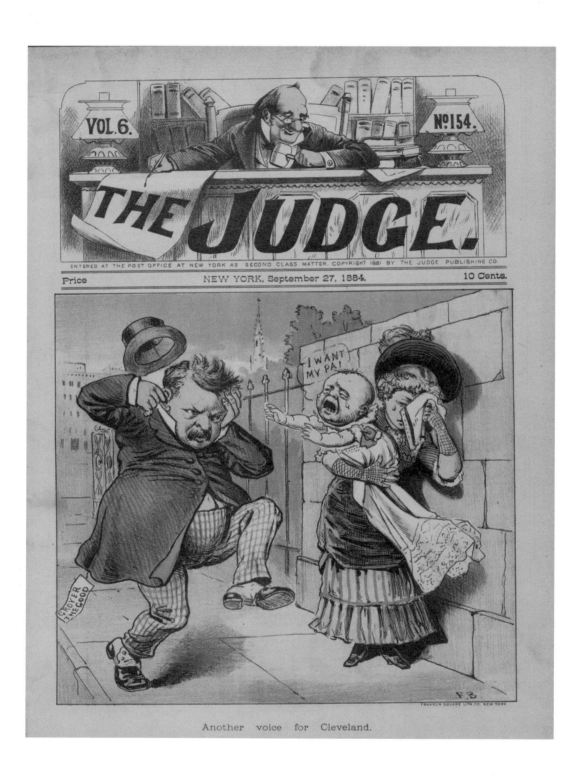

The Judge, *September 27, 1884 (fig. 7)*

Whether Cleveland had in his younger days fathered a child out of wedlock is not altogether certain. It may be that he had accepted paternity to protect a married friend. In any event, the charges of Cleveland's private indiscretion in the campaign of 1884 were balanced out by allegations of public corruption on the part of his Republican opponent, James G. Blaine.

Library of Congress

The Tattooed Man, Puck, *June 4, 1884 (fig. 8)*

Library of Congress

Throughout the campaign, cartoonists had a field day with both candidates. Thomas Nast excoriated Blaine with a series of drawings in *Harper's Weekly* that portrayed the Republican candidate as a self-aggrandizing politico interested largely in lining his own pockets, while a famous *Puck* cartoon pictured him as the tattooed man, a human tapestry detailing his public malfeasance *(fig. 8)*. Cleveland's "woman scrape" also proved good fodder for pictorial commentary, the most famous being a cartoon showing an infant bawling "I want my pa!" As the campaign progressed, it looked as if Cleveland's sexual indiscretion might trump Blaine's unsavory reputation as a "spoils man" and tilt the vote toward the Republican contender.

Scarcely a week before the election, however, a "perfect storm" of political happenstance conspired to undo Blaine's candidacy. The trouble began in New York at a meeting with several hundred Protestant ministers who had endorsed the Republican ticket. The group's spokesman guaranteed those present that "[we] don't propose to leave our party and identify ourselves with the party whose antecedents have been rum, Romanism, and rebellion."[11] Blaine failed to recognize the damage such a statement would do among New York City's large Irish Catholic community, to which the pejorative alliteration referred and which, in uncharacteristic fashion, was leaning toward supporting the Republican candidate. But the Democrats immediately saw the insult's significance and wasted no time in using it to virtually guarantee that Blaine's support among this important constituency would evaporate. Things got worse that evening when Blaine attended a lavish dinner hosted by the city's richest businessmen. Blaine appeared tone-deaf to the politically unwise note his presence at this elite gathering struck when sent to an electorate mired in a sharp economic downturn. Along with the anti-Irish slur, it proved enough to help lose New York State for him by less than 1,200 votes and to make his national defeat certain. In the days following the final election, Democrats thus took gleefully to answering the GOP's question of "Ma! Ma! Where's my Pa?" with "Gone to the White House, Ha! Ha! Ha!"

THE HAPPY WARRIOR AND THE GREAT ENGINEER

An embittered Al Smith, the defeated Democratic candidate for president in 1928, summed up his loss to Herbert Hoover with the observation that "the time hasn't come when a man can say his beads in the White House."[12] The issue of religion, long present in American presidential politics, took on central significance when Smith, the well-respected four-term reform Governor of New York, became the first Catholic candidate to run on a major party ticket. Smith's Republican opponent was Herbert Hoover, Secretary of Commerce to both Harding and Coolidge and the universally acclaimed manager of European food relief during World War I.

The American electorate had rarely, if ever, been presented with a candidate like Smith. The "Happy Warrior," as Franklin Roosevelt dubbed him at the 1924 Democratic convention, spoke with a distinct New York accent that served as a constant reminder of his Lower East Side origins *(fig. 9)*. A product of the Tammany Hall Democratic political machine, a devout Catholic, and a politician whose fondness for a drink flew in the face of the era's prohibition legislation, Smith was unabashedly urban in his interests and outlooks. Hoover, in contrast, was a native of Iowa who was orphaned at an early age and raised by relatives in Oregon. Trained as a mining engineer, he made his fortune at a young age before deciding to dedicate himself to public service *(fig. 10)*. His unblemished record of accomplishment and reputation as an adept manager made him a logical choice for the Republicans.

From the campaign's earliest days, the Democrats' primary challenge was to make Smith palatable to non-urban voters leery of his religion and his big-city ways. Although the United States had officially become an

Campaign pins for Al Smith, 1928 (fig. 9)

Campaign pins for Herbert Hoover, 1928 (fig. 10)

An Anti-Smith Campaign pin, 1928 (fig. 11)

urban nation in 1920, when the census recorded that more than 50% of all Americans lived in communities with 2,500 or more residents, an anti-urban bias remained quite strong among many American voters. And, no city was more urban than New York City, a place one editorial writer for the *Denver Post* declared was "a cesspool into which immigrant trash has been dumped for so long that it can scarcely be considered American anymore."[13] Believing that his legitimate credentials as a progressive reformer should trump concerns about his urban base and his religion, Smith and his supporters played up his New York roots and elected not to address the frequent attacks on his Catholicism throughout much of the campaign. This proved to be a major miscalculation. As absurd as concerns that Smith would bring the pope to the United States and install him in the White House may seem today to many Americans his devotion to his church became the election's major issue. Their suspicions were fanned by extremists such as members of the Ku Klux Klan as well as more moderate representatives of mainline Protestant churches and leading journalists of the day.

The virulence of many of the anti-Smith utterances harkened back to the Know-Nothings' fulminations against all things foreign in the 1840s. "If you vote for Al Smith you're voting against Christ and you'll be damned," roared one Baptist preacher *(fig. 11)*.[14] "Shall we have a man in the White House," asked Lutheran church leader Dr. Charles L. Fry, "who acknowledges allegiance to the Autocrat on the Tiber, who hates democracy, public schools, Protestant parsonages, individual right, and everything that is essential to independence?"[15] The generally temperate William Allen White, editor of *The Emporia Gazette* in Kansas and a supporter of Progressive politicians such as Robert M. La Follette, expressed a somewhat more nuanced but nonetheless damning critique of Smith's candidacy. While acknowledging Smith's considerable political skills, he editorialized it was "not that Governor Smith is a Catholic and a wet which makes him an offense to the villagers and town dwellers, but because his record shows the kind of president he would make—a Tammany President . . . [and] Tammany is Tammany and Smith is its prophet. The whole Puritan civilization which has built a sturdy, orderly nation is threatened by Smith."[16]

While Hoover appears not to have shared such sentiments, his condemnations of the anti-Catholicism rhetoric that characterized much of the campaign were tame and infrequent. He refused to debate Smith and never mentioned his name while campaigning, focusing instead on the Republican theme of prosperity. The 1928 campaign produced the Republican boast of "A chicken in every pot and two cars in every garage," and in his nomination acceptance speech Hoover had claimed that the United States was "in sight of the day when poverty will be banished from the nation."[17] Hoover, claimed his supporters, was a great engineer at the very moment when that was what the country needed most. The advertising pioneer Bruce Barton encapsulated the distinctions between the two candidates best when he wrote, "I might get more fun out of having Smith around, but I'd make more money with Hoover."[18]

The election was a Republican landslide: Hoover won by more than six million votes, and enjoyed a better than five-to-one margin of victory in the Electoral College (444 to 88). Even Smith's home state of New York went for Hoover. At bottom, although his religion proved to be his most insurmountable political liability, Smith also proved to be far too urban a man for many Americans. The political analyst Walter Lippmann captured this attitude when he wrote that opposition to Smith was "inspired by the feeling that the clamorous life of the city should not be acknowledged as the American ideal. . . . The Ku Kluxers may talk about the Pope to the lunatic fringe, but the main mass of the opposition is governed by an instinct that to accept Al Smith is to certify and sanctify a way of life that does not belong to the America they love."[19]

After Smith's resounding defeat, it would be 32 years until another Catholic stood for president. Unlike Smith, that candidate—John Kennedy—would confront the question of his religion head on. In a speech to the Greater Houston Ministerial Association on September 12, 1960, he declared, "I am not the Catholic candidate for President. I am the Democratic Party's candidate for President who also happens to be a Catholic. I do not speak for my Church on public matters — and the Church does not speak for me."[20]

As mentioned at the outset, the contests of 1828, 1884, and 1928 are but three examples of how accusatory mudslinging, appeals to bias, and negative innuendo have played a significant part in past presidential elections. And as long as there are White House hopefuls, we can be assured that such tactics will continue to be enlisted to shape voter opinion. For assurance of that, there is no need to look farther than the primary season of 2008. Whether it was the Mormonism of Mitt Romney, the complicated personal life of Rudolph Giuliani, or the complex political and personal dynamics of Hillary Clinton's years as first lady, it is abundantly clear that there are legions of partisans across America eagerly contriving new spins on such factors that will redound to the benefit of their own candidates.

Endnotes

1 "howling atheist" in Evan Cornog and Richard Whalen, *Hats in the Ring: An Illustrated History of American Presidential Campaigns* (New York: Random House, 2000), p. 21.

2 "howl of democracy" in Paul Boller, *Presidential Campaigns: From George Washington to George W. Bush* (New York: Oxford University Press, 2004), p. 42.

3 "dogmatically and systematically repulsive . . ." in Carter Smith, *Presidents: Every Question Answered* (New York: Hylas Publications, 2004), p. 52.

4 "The ABC. . .," Boller, *Presidential Campaigns,* p. 50

5 "Those vile wretches . . . " in Stefan Lorant, *The Glorious Burden: The History of the Presidency and Presidential Elections from George Washington to James Earl Carter, Jr.* (Lenox, Massachusetts: Author's Edition, Inc., 1976), p. 126.

6 "the coming political campaign . . ." in *ibid.*, p. 369.

7 "delinquent in office but blameless . . . ," Allan Nevins quoted in Boller, *Presidential Campaigns,* p. 146

8 "wallowed in spoils . . . " in Lorant, *The Glorious Burden,* p. 377.

9 "Gentlemen, you have been misinformed. . . ." in Arthur M. Schlesinger, Jr., ed., *Running for President: The Candidates and Their Images, 1789-1896,* vol. I (New York: Simon & Schuster, 1994), p. 371.

10 Schlesinger, vol. I, *passim*.

11 ". . . rum, Romanism, and rebellion" in Boller, *Presidential Campaigns*, p. 149.

12 "the time hasn't come . . ." in Christopher M. Finan, *Alfred E. Smith: The Happy Warrior* (New York: Hill and Wang, 2003), p. 230.

13 *Ibid.*, p. 189.

14 "If you vote for Al Smith . . ." in Lorant, *The Glorious Burden,* p. 579.

15 " . . .the Autocrat on the Tiber . . ." in Finan, *Alfred E. Smith,* p. 210.

16 "not that Governor Smith is a Catholic and a wet . . ." in Lorant, *The Glorious Burden,* p. 581.

17 "A chicken in every pot . . ." in *ibid.*, p. 578.

18 "I might get more fun . . ." in Bolling, *Presidential Campaigns,* p. 227.

19 ". . . The Klu Kluxers may talk about the Pope . . ." in Finan, *Alfred E. Smith,* p. 192.

20 "I am not the Catholic candidate. . . ." in Robert Dallek, *An Unfinished Life: John F. Kennedy, 1917 - 1963* (Boston: Back Bay Books, 2004), p. 564.

PROGRESSIVE CANDIDATE FOR PRESIDENT

THE MAN OF THE HOUR

ROOSEVELT

An Era of
Traditions Spurned
1912-1960

Beginning with the election of 1912, a number of long established traditions in presidential politics went by the boards. While not the first time that a former president ran on a third party ticket—Millard Fillmore was the American (Know-Nothing) Party candidate in 1856—the 1912 election was the first and only time that a former occupant of the Oval Office running on a third party ticket outpolled the mainstream candidate of his former party. Theodore Roosevelt's insurgent Bull Moose campaign, while failing to carry him to the White House, did bear primary responsibility for unseating Republican incumbent William Howard Taft, TR's chosen successor four years earlier.

A second third party candidate in 1912, the oft-nominated Socialist Eugene Debs, attracted over 900,000 votes eight years later while serving a sentence in Atlanta's federal penitentiary for opposing the First World War. His vote count represented a high water mark for his party: even the six-time Socialist candidate Norman Thomas, who contested each presidential election between 1928 and 1948, never attracted more votes. And, no candidate before or since Debs has run for the nation's highest office while in prison.

In 1932, a second Roosevelt, TR's fifth cousin Franklin Delano Roosevelt, was elected to the first of his precedent-shattering four terms in office. That extraordinary electoral success led to bitter resentments among Republicans who eventually spearheaded the passage of the 22nd amendment stating that "No person shall be elected to the office of the President more than twice, and no person who has held the office of President, or acted as President, for more than two years of a term to which some other person was elected President shall be elected to the office of the President more than once." Ironically, this amendment held unintended consequences for its Republican sponsors. While it may indeed prevent any future FDRs, many in both parties presume that Republican Ronald Reagan could well have run successfully for a third term in 1988 had the amendment not existed.

1912
A Bull Moose Enters the Fray

After nearly two full terms in the presidency, Theodore Roosevelt cheerfully turned the White House over to his hand-picked successor, William Howard Taft, in 1909. But Roosevelt soon came to see Taft's administration as a betrayal of his own presidency, and by early 1912 was openly vying with Taft for the Republican presidential nomination. Taft won that battle, but Roosevelt had come too far to retire gracefully. Convinced that Taft's followers had cheated him out of the GOP endorsement, he was soon mounting a third party candidacy under the banner of the newly formed Progressive Party. Nicknamed the Bull Moose Party after Roosevelt likened his health to that most robust of animals, the Progressives had two main assets—a reform agenda that fit the prevailing political mood, and the charismatic exuberance of Roosevelt himself. That was enough to kill Taft's chances for re-election. But it was not enough to win against Democratic hopeful Woodrow Wilson. While Taft finished a distant third in the final tally, Roosevelt in turn trailed Wilson by a good deal in the popular vote and even more in the Electoral College.

Theodore Roosevelt, Progressive Party

Roosevelt's Bull Moose logo was one of the most colorful aspects of the 1912 presidential contest. Equally memorable was the unmincing self-righteousness of some of his campaign utterances. "Thou shalt not steal!" he had railed following his loss of the Republican presidential nomination to Taft. Several weeks later, he again waxed biblical, telling the attendees at the Progressive Party convention that "We stand at Armageddon, and we battle for the Lord."

Campaign Results

Election Year	Candidate	Office	Party	Electoral Vote	Popular Vote
1912	Woodrow Wilson	P	Democratic	435	6,296,547
	Thomas R. Marshall	VP			
	William H. Taft	P	Republican	8	3,486,720
	James S. Sherman	VP			
	Theodore Roosevelt		Progressive	88	4,118,571
	Eugene V. Debs		Socialist	--	900,672
	Eugene W. Chafin		Prohibition	--	206,275

1916
He Kept Us Out of War

The re-election of Woodrow Wilson was hardly guaranteed. Although he had pre-empted the Progressive agenda by adopting many of the reforms championed by Theodore Roosevelt and others, the threat that America might be drawn into the war in Europe was of growing concern to many voters. Hoping for a return to the White House, Roosevelt stumped hard for the Republican nomination with calls for America's immediate entry into the war. But his break with the party four years earlier had soured his relationships with the party's leaders, who turned instead to Charles Hughes, a sitting justice on the U. S. Supreme Court. The ensuing campaign revolved around which candidate might best avoid entanglement in the European conflict. The Democrats made much of the claim that "He kept us out of war." Meanwhile Hughes had to contend with the bellicose TR's constant saber-rattling and faint-hearted support of the Republican ticket. Despite these difficulties, many voters (Hughes included) went to bed on election night thinking that Hughes had won, but a margin of just over 3,000 votes in California gave the state and the presidency to Wilson.

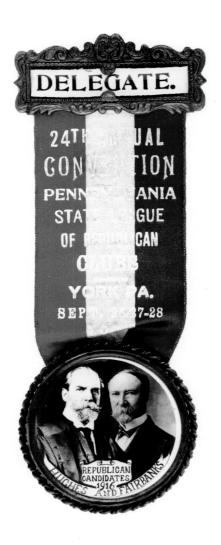

Campaign Results

Election Year	Candidate	Office	Party	Electoral Vote	Popular Vote
1916	Woodrow Wilson	P	Democratic	277	9,127,695
	Thomas R. Marshall	VP			
	Charles E. Hughes	P	Republican	254	8,533,507
	Charles W. Fairbanks	VP			
	A.L. Benson		Socialist	--	585,113
	J. Frank Hanly		Prohibition	--	220,506

1920
A Return to Normalcy

By 1920, the popular enthusiasm for economic and social reform that had been driving the country's legislative agenda for several years was nearly dead. World War I had recently ended, and voters wanted no more new crusades, domestic or otherwise. The presidential hopeful that year who seemed most likely to accommodate that wish was the Republicans' Warren G. Harding, a onetime small town newspaper editor and a sitting senator from Ohio. Harding had little to recommend him for the nation's highest office. But as pundits of the day noted, his white hair and chiseled features made him look presidential, and with his gift for talking in nearly meaningless generalities about a "return to normalcy," he offered the sort of unchallenging comfort that the electorate craved. On Election Day, his victory over Democrat James Cox was an unprecedented landslide, with Harding claiming over 60 percent of the popular votes, which for the first time included those of the nation's recently enfranchised female populace.

James Cox

Unlike his Republican opponent Warren Harding, Democratic presidential hopeful James Cox spoke to voters of a need for continuing domestic reform. He also defended the hope of Woodrow Wilson's current Democratic administration that the United States would join the new League of Nations founded under the terms of the treaty ending World War I. In so doing, Cox was bucking an overwhelming tide against change and any new foreign adventures. Many of his campaign utterances made Harding's empty talk of "cultivating friendliness and neighborliness" seem all the more appealing.

Campaign Results

Election Year	Candidate	Office	Party	Electoral Vote	Popular Vote
1920	Warren G. Harding	P	Republican	404	16,143,407
	Calvin Coolidge	VP			
	James M. Cox	P	Democratic	127	9,130,328
	Franklin D. Roosevelt	VP			
	Eugene V. Debs		Socialist	--	919,799
	P.P. Christensen		Farmer Labor	--	265,411
	Aaron S. Watkins		Prohibition	--	189,408

1924
A Win for "Silent" Cal

Vice President Calvin Coolidge succeeded to the White House upon the death of Harding in September 1923, and the following year found himself campaigning for the presidency in his own right. The recent disclosures of serious corruption in Harding's administration might have hurt his chances of winning had it not been for his own unassailable honesty. Dubbed "Silent Cal"—a nickname inspired by his reputation as a man of few words—Coolidge also had the very decided advantage of presiding over a thriving economy. The nation's mounting prosperity made his November victory over his Democratic opponent John Davis an almost foregone conclusion.

John W. Davis in 1924

At their 1924 convention, the Democrats were deadlocked for well over a week. It was not until the one hundred and third ballot that dark horse John W. Davis finally claimed the nomination. A lawyer and former solicitor-general under Woodrow Wilson, Davis faced an uphill battle in an election year when a booming economy so heavily favored the re-election of the incumbent, Calvin Coolidge. It became harder yet when the GOP simply ignored Davis's attacks on the Republican administration, in effect turning him into the campaign's forgotten man. In his frustration he complained: "If scandals break out in the government, the way to treat them is— silence. If petted industries make extortionate profits under an extortionate tariff, the answer is—silence."

Robert La Follette, Progressive Party

The nation's growing prosperity during the 1920s was beginning to persuade many that poverty in America might soon become a thing of the past and that there was no need for government to take a hand in regulating a booming economy. But some thought otherwise. Chief among the contrarians was Robert La Follette, the Progressive Party's presidential candidate of 1924. A founder of the Progressive movement many years earlier, this ex-governor and sitting senator from Wisconsin firmly believed that there was still a good deal that government could do to improve the lot of ordinary workers and farmers. In the face of the country's complacency, La Follette's chances of winning the White House were nil. Nevertheless, his hard-driving style added a good deal of color to the contest. "Unfortunately, for romance," an admirer once observed, "La Follette was caught young, and civilized. What a pirate or highwayman might this barrel of wild cats have made! What a swashbuckling Dumas hero!"

Campaign Results

Election Year	Candidate	Office	Party	Electoral Vote	Popular Vote
1924	Calvin Coolidge	P	Republican	382	15,718,211
	Charles G. Dawes	VP			
	John W. Davis	P	Democratic	136	8,385,283
	Charles W. Bryan	VP			
	Robert M. La Follette		Progressive	13	4,831,289

1928

The Engineer and the Happy Warrior

With the electorate crediting Calvin Coolidge's Republican administration for the country's current booming prosperity, even a weak GOP presidential candidate would have been almost certain of winning in 1928. As it was, the Republicans had quite a strong candidate in Herbert Hoover. Admittedly, he was none too exciting a personality. But as a self-made multi-millionaire who had shown himself to be a masterful manager in both the private and public sector, he struck many as the ideal choice for maintaining the nation's soaring economy. On Election Day, he claimed a landslide victory over former New York governor Al Smith, the "Happy Warrior" who was easily one of the Democratic Party's most personable leaders.

A "Christian in the White House"

As the Democrats' White House standard bearer of 1928, New York's Al Smith had significant vulnerabilities. While his call for Prohibition's repeal alienated the nation's "dry" contingency, his associations with New York's Tammany machine raised questions in some minds about his honesty. But perhaps Smith's greatest liability was his Catholicism, which fostered fear among many Protestants that his election to the White House would introduce Papal influence into the nation's affairs. That fear sometimes expressed itself quite directly. One Protestant minister told his congregation that voting for Smith meant certain damnation. But other times the message was more subtly delivered, as was the case with a pin calling for a "Christian in the White House." In the campaign parlance of 1928, "Christian" meant non Catholic

Campaign Results

Election Year	Candidate	Office	Party	Electoral Vote	Popular Vote
1928	Herbert C. Hoover	P	Republican	444	21,391,993
	Charles Curtis	VP			
	Alfred E. Smith	P	Democratic	87	15,016,169
	Joseph T. Robinson	VP			
	Norman Thomas		Socialist	--	267,835

1932
The Politics
of the Great Depression

By 1932 the country was suffering through the worst economic downturn in its history. The stock market, which had reached an all-time high in 1929, had lost over eighty percent of its value. With the ranks of the unemployed numbering in the many millions and still growing, urban breadlines often ran for blocks. Even many of the more comfortably fixed were not immune to the suffering as a steady stream of bank failures wiped out their entire savings. Against this backdrop of a depression which persisted into the late 1930s, the outcomes of the presidential campaigns in both 1932 and 1936 hinged on which party seemed to offer the best way out of this economic nightmare. While Republicans argued that government's capacity to mend the problems was limited, Democrats promised a "New Deal" activism in regulating the nation's economic affairs. In both contests, the electorate opted overwhelmingly for that activism.

Franklin Delano Roosevelt, Democrat

In his bid for the presidency in 1932, Democrat Franklin Roosevelt promised the nation a "New Deal." When it came to defining this catchphrase, however, neither he nor his supporters ever ventured much beyond vague generalities. Still, the term had a ring that engendered hope, and in the midst of ever deepening depression that was enough to satisfy the electorate, which elected Roosevelt in a landslide. But a New Deal was not the only thing that Roosevelt and his running mate, the Texan John Nance Garner, were offering the country. The campaign license plate above, featuring a full mug of beer, was meant to remind voters that they also favored repeal of the Constitution's Eighteenth Amendment imposing prohibition of alcoholic beverages.

Herbert Hoover's Re-election Bid, 1932

At the outset of his presidency in 1929, Herbert Hoover had predicted that America's soaring economy would soon make poverty a thing of the past. Unfortunately, over the next four years, poverty became ever more prevalent as the nation plunged into the worst depression in its history. Although Hoover instituted a number of important measures to ease the situation, his lack of personal warmth made him seem indifferent to the nation's suffering. In response to that perceived indifference, the clusters of makeshift shacks springing up across the country to house the growing ranks of homeless became known as "Hoovervilles." Once hailed as a brilliant man who could do anything he set his mind to, Hoover now struck many as woefully inept. Even as his fellow Republicans nominated him to run for a second term, they knew that his chances of winning were all but non-existent.

Norman Thomas, Socialist Party

Once likening the country's two major parties to "identical bottles with different labels and both empty," Socialist Norman Thomas ran for the presidency six times. Even in the Great Depression, when dire circumstances pushed many people toward the more extreme ends of the political spectrum, voter attraction to his cause was insignificant. Nevertheless, his reforming activism helped give currency to many ideas—among them old-age pensions and unemployment insurance—that eventually found their way into mainstream political thinking.

Campaign Results

Election Year	Candidate	Office	Party	Electoral Vote	Popular Vote
1932	Franklin D. Roosevelt	P	Democratic	472	22,809,638
	John Nance Garner	VP			
	Herbert C. Hoover	P	Republican	59	15,758,901
	Charles Curtis	VP			
	Norman Thomas		Socialist	--	881,951
	William Z. Foster		Communist	--	102,785
	William D. Upshaw		Prohibition	--	81,869

1936
Alf Landon
for the Republicans

At their national convention in 1936, the Republicans drew up a platform characterizing the economic reforms and public works projects instituted by Franklin Roosevelt's New Deal administration as "misdeeds and usurpations" that were placing "America in peril." To rescue the country from these dangers, they designated Kansas Governor Alf Landon as their choice to defeat Roosevelt's re-election. Although Landon's claim to the "Sunflower State" gave his campaign a distinct edge when it came to producing eye-catching advertising, a solid majority of Americans remained firmly convinced that the New Deal held the answers to economic recovery. In the final count Landon managed to win only Maine and Vermont.

Campaign Results

Election Year	Candidate	Office	Party	Electoral Vote	Popular Vote
1936	Franklin D. Roosevelt	P	Democratic	523	27,752,869
	John Nance Garner	VP			
	Alfred M. Landon	P	Republican	8	16,674,665
	Frank Knox	VP			
	William Lemke		Union	--	882,479
	Norman Thomas		Socialist	--	187,720
	Earl Browder		Communist	--	80,159

1940
An Unprecedented Third Term

The backers of Wendell Willkie, the Republican White House hopeful in 1940, had a unique weapon in their campaign to defeat incumbent Franklin Roosevelt. Ever since George Washington, no president had served more than two terms, but now Roosevelt was seeking a third term. Although there was nothing in the Constitution to stop him, the Republicans painted Roosevelt's re-election bid as a horrendous breach of American political custom and a precursor to dictatorship. As a result, some of the most widely worn campaign pins among Republicans in 1940 were those declaring "no third term" for Roosevelt. The majority of voters, however, did not buy the no-third-term argument. In their eyes, Roosevelt's New Deal had rescued them from the Depression, and with international events now threatening to draw the country into World War II, his proven credentials for handling crises made him much more preferable than Willkie.

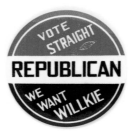

FDR Bucks Tradition

Despite claims that Roosevelt's New Deal had pretty much solved the problems of the Great Depression, hindsight makes it clear that FDR's eight years in office had fallen well short of that goal. Nevertheless, the perception that Roosevelt had rescued the country from disaster was widespread among the electorate. Voters' positive views of the New Deal were so strong, in fact, that Roosevelt's Republican opponent, Wendell Willkie, felt compelled to soft pedal his criticisms to such an extent that he sometimes sounded a bit like a Roosevelt backer. After listening to one of Willkie's major campaign statements, one journalist observed: "All I got from that speech was an endorsement of the New Deal."

Campaign Results

Election Year	Candidate	Office	Party	Electoral Vote	Popular Vote
1940	Franklin D. Roosevelt	P	Democratic	449	27,307,819
	Henry A. Wallace	VP			
	Wendell L. Willkie	P	Republican	82	22,321,018
	Charles McNary	VP			
	Norman Thomas		Socialist	--	99,557

1944
No Change Amidst War

By the end of his third term, Franklin Roosevelt was eager to retire, worn down by the pressures of wartime leadership and in poor health. Nevertheless, he accepted his party's nomination for an unprecedented fourth term and lobbied successfully for the selection of Missouri Senator Harry Truman as his running mate. The Republicans turned to Thomas Dewey, the young governor of New York who had made his reputation first as a federal prosecutor and then as the Manhattan district attorney. There were few policy issues separating the two parties. The Republicans were generally supportive of the New Deal programs, and the parties shared a commitment to the national unity necessary to prosecute the war effort. Dewey sought instead to capitalize on FDR's run for a fourth term and on the president's health and age, arguing that a new generation of leaders was necessary to make the government function more efficiently. Initially determined not to campaign in traditional fashion, Roosevelt waited until well into the election cycle before entering the political arena in response to what he considered an unfair set of personal attacks. His efforts were likely not needed, for the American voters gave him a landslide victory.

Campaign Results

Election Year	Candidate	Office	Party	Electoral Vote	Popular Vote
1944	Franklin D. Roosevelt	P	Democratic	432	25,606,585
	Harry S. Truman	VP			
	Thomas E. Dewey	P	Republican	99	22,014,745
	John Bricker	VP			
	Norman Thomas		Socialist	--	80,518

1948
Confounding the Pollsters

Even before the presidential campaign went into full swing in 1948, polls made it abundantly clear that Republican hopeful Thomas Dewey had the distinct edge. Indeed, the Democrats appeared so severely fractured over civil rights and Cold War policy toward the Soviet Union that their incumbent candidate Harry Truman seemed to be engaging in a futile exercise when he launched his campaign train tour in September. One poll had declared Dewey "unbeatable," and even as Truman's whistle-stop speechmaking began drawing crowds by the many thousands, the predictions remained the same. By Election Day, not one columnist or pollster in the entire country thought Truman had even a faint chance of winning. But clearly the experts had greatly underestimated the enormous appeal of Truman's gritty, hard-hitting stump style. On the morning of the day following the election, a somewhat flabbergasted nation awoke to the news that Truman, who only days earlier had been written off as a "Study in Failure," had won.

Dewey Wins?

This photograph captures what must have been for Truman one of the sweetest moments of his surprise victory of 1948. Under the management of the rabidly Republican Robert McCormick, the *Chicago Tribune* had confidently declared the president's political demise before all the polling results were known. It doubtless gave Truman great satisfaction to brandish an early post-election edition. As he held the paper up before a crowd of well-wishers, he counseled: "Don't believe everything you read in the newspapers."

Harry Truman, 1948

Truman's chances of winning the election of 1948 were thought to be so dim that reporters often found it hard to believe how the candidate himself could continue to think otherwise. After a conversation with Truman, during which he confidently predicted victory, one correspondent speculated that he was simply "putting on the most magnificent and fighting front of optimism" ever exhibited by a sure-to-lose candidate.

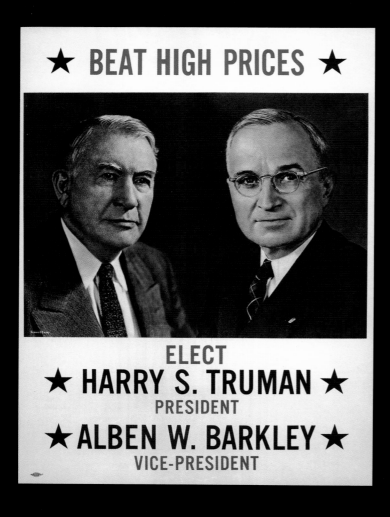

Thomas Dewey, 1948

Although Thomas Dewey seemed to be a White House shoo-in, experts overlooked several factors when they so confidently predicted his November victory. His cool and somewhat aloof manner and the excessively tight orchestration of his every campaign appearance, down to what hat his wife could wear, made him less appealing than his Democratic opponent. Dewey's lack of warmth and spontaneity put Alice Roosevelt Longworth in mind of "the groom on a wedding cake" and may have gone a long way in explaining why the electorate ultimately gravitated to the more natural, down-to-earth Truman.

Henry Wallace, Progressive Party

Henry Wallace had long been a stalwart supporter of the Democratic cause, and had served both as Franklin Roosevelt's Secretary of Agriculture and vice president. His belief that the best path to world peace lay in closer cooperation in the face of mounting Cold War tensions between the Soviet Union and the United States following World War II, however, made Wallace an outspoken critic of President Truman's adversarial strategies for dealing with Soviet expansionism. In 1948, Wallace deserted the Democratic Party to challenge Truman's presidential bid with his own White House candidacy on the Progressive ticket. In the face of mounting popular anxiety over Soviet influence in the world, Wallace's call for more conciliatory policies held little appeal for the electorate, and his candidacy attracted far fewer voters than he had hoped.

Campaign Results

Election Year	Candidate	Office	Party	Electoral Vote	Popular Vote
1948	Harry S. Truman	P	Democratic	303	24,105,812
	Alben Barkley	VP			
	Thomas E. Dewey	P	Republican	189	21,970,065
	Earl Warren	VP			
	Strom Thurmond		States' Rights	39	1,169,063
	Henry Wallace		Progressive	--	1,157,172
	Norman Thomas		Socialist	--	139,414
	Claude A. Watson		Prohibition	--	103,224

1952 & 1956
We Like Ike (twice)

In the White House contest of 1952, the Republicans held just about every advantage any party could. Charged with mismanaging the Korean War and losing China to Communism, Harry Truman's Democratic administration also stood accused of corruption and tolerating Soviet infiltration into high government circles. As Republican operatives liked to say, the winning formula in this election year boiled down to K1C2—Korea, Corruption, and Communism. But every bit as valuable as that trio of attack targets was the GOP's presidential standard bearer, Dwight Eisenhower. As the general who had orchestrated victory in the European theater during World War II, Eisenhower was already one of the most popular figures in America. Furthermore, he came to his candidacy armed with a broad grin and engaging common touch that were all but irresistible. In the presidential election where television for the first time played an important role, his easy warmth became a crucial factor in accounting for his decisive November landslide over the Democrats' Adlai Stevenson.

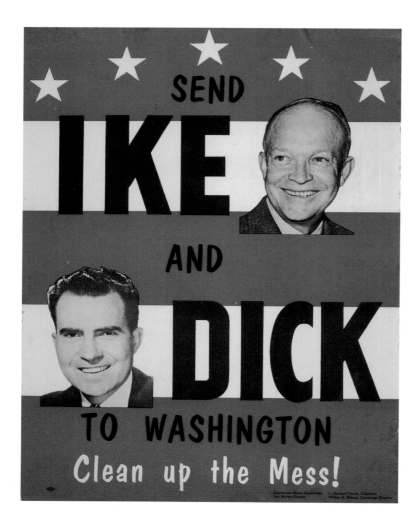

Adlai Stevenson, 1952

"Ike," the nickname of Republican hopeful Dwight Eisenhower, quickly gave birth to "I Like Ike." As the phrase gained ever wider currency during the 1952 campaign, the Democrats felt compelled to come up with an equally snappy declaration of enthusiasm for their own White House hopeful, Adlai Stevenson. They ultimately hit on such phrases as "Madly for Adlai" and "We Need Adlai Badly." But the Democrats also needed a counterpoint to the famously appealing Eisenhower grin. One answer was this poster featuring a vibrantly smiling Stevenson. Unfortunately, grinning posters and catchy phrases could not outweigh Stevenson's tendency to intellectualize on the stump. While some voters found the thoughtful gravity of his speeches a refreshing change from the usual election-year rhetoric, the majority of the electorate remained unmoved, and his appearances often did little to enlarge popular enthusiasm for his candidacy.

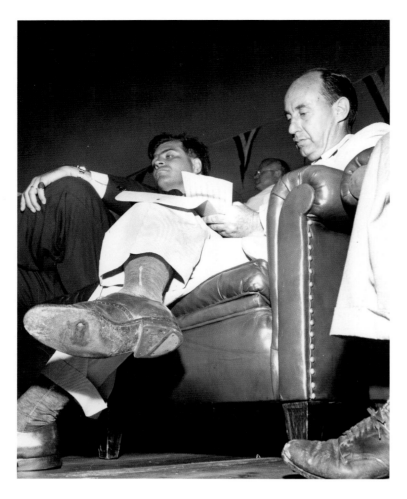

Stevenson's Holey Shoe

During the 1952 campaign, a photographer from Michigan's *Flint Journal* named William Gallagher suddenly spotted the opportunity for a shot that was a little out of the ordinary. Looking up at White House hopeful Adlai Stevenson seated on a stage, he soon focused his lens on Stevenson's feet, and the resulting picture revealed a hole in the sole of the candidate's right shoe. The photo ran in publications across the country, won Gallagher a Pulitzer Prize, and may also have helped to advance Stevenson's cause. Here, indeed, was an image that both humanized him and underscored the earnest sincerity of his candidacy. "I'm too engrossed in my cause" it seemed to say, "to worry about such trivialities as the sad state of my shoes."

Abraham Lincoln Presidential Library and Museum

Campaign Results

Election Year	Candidate	Office	Party	Electoral Vote	Popular Vote
1952	Dwight D. Eisenhower	P	Republican	442	33,936,234
	Richard Nixon	VP			
	Adlai Stevenson	P	Democratic	89	27,314,992
	John Sparkman	VP			
	Vincent Hallinan		Progressive	--	140,023
1956	Dwight D. Eisenhower	P	Republican	457	35,590,472
	Richard Nixon	VP			
	Adlai Stevenson	P	Democratic	73	26,022,752
	Estes Kefauver	VP			
	T. Coleman Andrews		States' Rights	--	107,929

The Electronic Candidate Since 1960

By the 1960s, the packaging of presidential candidates was changing rapidly and dramatically. The reason was quite simple—television. What had been a novelty in the early 1950s quickly became a significant part of everyday American life. By 1960, 85% of American homes had television sets, and in that same year, the first televised debates took place. Debates have a long tradition in American politics. In 1858, Abraham Lincoln and Stephen Douglas debated in their race for the U.S. Senate in Illinois. In their competition for the Republican presidential nomination in 1948, Thomas Dewey and Harold Stassen debated on the radio, and in 1956, Democratic hopefuls Adlai Stevenson and Estes Kefauver debated each other on television.

But never had the two major party's candidates for the presidency publicly faced each other to argue the issues. On September 26, 1960, this time-honored tradition was swept aside when the Democratic hopeful John F. Kennedy and his Republican opponent, Vice President Richard Nixon, engaged in the first, and perhaps the most significant, televised presidential debate. While those who had seen the debate on television overwhelmingly thought that Kennedy had won, the majority who had heard the exchange on radio thought Nixon had gotten the better of his opponent. While there would be three subsequent debates in 1960, this first face-to-face exchange established that visual impact can be as crucial in winning votes as message.

After 1960, there were no presidential debates until 1976, when the Democratic nominee is generally considered to have bested the incumbent, Gerald Ford. Despite some memorable moments, such as Ronald Reagan adroitly deflecting concerns about his age in 1984 by announcing, "I will not make age an issue of this campaign. I am not going to exploit, for political purposes, my opponent's [the 56-year-old Walter Mondale] youth and inexperience," television debates have become almost routine over the past two decades. Candidates now arrive at these face-offs heavily prepped, ready for almost any question, and armed with a few carefully chosen lines intended to make headlines in tomorrow's news.

The presidential contest between John F. Kennedy and Richard Nixon also marked the launching of the first full-blown television presidential advertising campaign. Since this beginning, the ways that presidential candidates are packaged continues to change with each election cycle. But the primacy of television and, more recently, of other electronic means of campaigning has not forestalled the use of more traditional forms of political persuasion to attract votes. Many of the posters and buttons produced in the last fifty years adopt graphic imagery that is little different from that used in campaigns of the 19th and early 20th centuries. Dramatic departures such as the posters supporting the candidacies of Richard Nixon, George McGovern, and Ross Perot shown on the following pages prove to be the exception. The production of campaign buttons has become an increasingly commercial venture. Driven less by the needs of a specific campaign than by a desire to sell to all comers, it is not unusual to encounter a bin of lapel buttons in any airport gift shop from which, for a few dollars, you can select your choice as the next president.

1960

Campaign Results

Election Year	Candidate	Office	Party	Electoral Vote	Popular Vote
1960	John F. Kennedy	P	Democratic	303	34,226,731
	Lyndon B. Johnson	VP			
	Richard M. Nixon	P	Republican	219	34,108,157
	Henry Cabot Lodge	VP			
1964	Lyndon B. Johnson	P	Democratic	486	43,129,484
	Hubert H. Humphrey	VP			
	Barry M. Goldwater	P	Republican	52	27,178,188
	William E. Miller	VP			
1968	Richard Nixon	P	Republican	301	31,770,237
	Spiro T. Agnew	VP			
	Hubert H. Humphrey	P	Democrat	191	31,270,533
	Edmund Muskie	VP			
	George C. Wallace		Independent	46	9,906,141
1972	Richard Nixon	P	Republican	521	46,631,189
	Spiro T. Agnew	VP			
	George McGovern	P	Democrat	17	28,422,015
	R. Sargent Shriver	VP			
1976	James Carter	P	Democrat	297	40,276,040
	Walter Mondale	VP			
	Gerald R. Ford	P	Republican	241	38,532,630
	Robert Dole	VP			
1980	Ronald Reagan	P	Republican	489	43,899,248
	George H.W. Bush	VP			
	James Carter	P	Democrat	49	35,481,435
	Walter Mondale	VP			
	John Anderson		Independent	0	5,719,437
1984	Ronald Reagan	P	Republican	525	53,354,037
	George H.W. Bush	VP			
	Walter Mondale	P	Democrat	13	36,884,260
	Geraldine Ferraro	VP			
1988	George H.W. Bush	P	Republican	426	47,946,422
	Dan Quayle	VP			
	Michael Dukakis	P	Democrat	112	41,016,429
	Lloyd Bentsen	VP			
1992	William J. Clinton	P	Democrat	370	43,682,624
	Al Gore	VP			
	George H.W. Bush	P	Republican	168	38,117,331
	Dan Quayle	VP			
	Ross Perot		Independent	0	19,217,213
1996	William J. Clinton	P	Democrat	379	45,628,667
	Al Gore	VP			
	Robert Dole	P	Republican	159	37,869,435
	Jack Kemp	VP			
	Ross Perot		Independent	0	7,874,283
2000	George W. Bush	P	Republican	271	50,459,211
	Dick Cheney	VP			
	Albert Gore	P	Democrat	267	51,003,894
	Joe Lieberman	VP			
	Ralph Nader		Green Party	0	2,834,410
	Patrick Buchanan		Reform Party	0	446,743
2004	George W. Bush	P	Republican	286	62,040,610
	Dick Cheney	VP			
	John F. Kerry	P	Democrat	251	59,028,444
	John Edwards	VP			
	Ralph Nader		Independent	0	465,650

THE ELECTRONIC CANDIDATE

DEBATES AND COMMERCIALS

Michael Cheney

By the 1960s, the packaging of the

PRESIDENCY WAS CHANGING RAPIDLY AND DRAMATICALLY, AND IN A FEW SHORT YEARS, IT WOULD BE FOREVER TRANSFORMED. THE REASON WAS QUITE SIMPLE—TELEVISION HAD REACHED A TIPPING POINT. WHAT HAD STILL BEEN A NOVELTY IN THE EARLY 1950S QUICKLY BECAME A SIGNIFICANT PART OF EVERYDAY LIFE OVER THE NEXT DECADE. WITH TELEVISION, VIEWERS GOT TO SEE EVERYTHING LIVE. THEY COULD WATCH THE HEARINGS OF SENATOR JOSEPH MCCARTHY LOOKING FOR COMMUNIST SYMPATHIZERS IN THE U.S. GOVERNMENT OR WATCH THE MACARTHUR DAY PARADE IN CHICAGO WHERE TELEVISION VIEWERS FELT MORE ENGAGED THAN THOSE ATTENDING THE EVENT, OR WATCH DON LARSEN THROW A PERFECT GAME IN THE 1956 WORLD SERIES.

During the 1950s, politics had slowly come to terms with television. In 1952, the first presidential television commercial was aired, and the nominating conventions were shown nationwide. Probably the most dramatic political event of the 1950s took place that same year when vice-presidential candidate Richard Nixon "took his case to the people" through television to defend himself against charges of corruption in what became known as the "Checkers" speech.[1] *(fig. 1)*

Yet the quiz show scandals of the late 1950s brought disgrace to the new medium, and the government review of the scandal quickly brought renewed attention to what was being done with the public airwaves. In response, the three television networks chose to use the 1960 presidential campaign to showcase television at its best.

It was a watershed year for television and politics. By then 85% of American homes had television sets, and in that same year, the first televised debates took place.[2] Nineteen-sixty also marked the launching of the first full-blown television presidential advertising campaign. Since this beginning, the ways that presidential candidates are packaged continues to change with each election cycle. But the primacy of television as a vehicle for shaping an election's outcome has remained constant.

TELEVISED PRESIDENTIAL DEBATES

Debates have a long tradition in American politics. In 1858, Abraham Lincoln and Stephen Douglas debated in their race for the U.S. Senate in Illinois. In their competition for the Republican presidential nomination in 1948, Thomas Dewey and Harold Stassen debated on the radio, and in 1956, Democratic hopefuls Adlai Stevenson and Estes Kefauver debated each other on television. But never, in more than a century and a half of presidential campaigning, had the two major parties' candidates for the presidency publicly faced each other to argue the issues. On September 26, 1960, however, that time-honored tradition was swept aside when the Democratic hopeful John F. Kennedy and his Republican opponent, Vice President Richard Nixon, engaged in the first, and perhaps the most significant, televised presidential debate.[3]

Held in the studios of WBBM-TV in Chicago, the debate was carried live on all three networks. While much was said during the debate, what was not said turned out to be the most telling. Kennedy had arrived at the debate from a campaign swing through California and looked tanned and fresh, wearing a dark suit. Nixon had been ill and was recuperating from a knee injury. He looked pale. In an effort to correct the situation, his

Vice presidential nominee Richard Nixon gives his "Checkers" speech, 1952 (fig. 1)

AP Images

advisers took him into a backroom and, unaided by a television makeup artist, performed a quick makeup job that did little to mask his sickly look. Further, Nixon's carefully chosen gray suit—this was the age of black and white television—matched the studio backdrop and gave the impression that he was blending into the scenery.[4] *(fig. 2)*

In polls following the debate, those who had seen it on television overwhelmingly thought that Kennedy had won over Nixon. Interestingly enough, however, the majority of those who had heard the exchange on radio thought Nixon had won. While there would be three subsequent debates in 1960, this first face-to-face exchange established a new axiom for presidential campaigning in the age of television: visual impact can be as crucial in winning votes as message.[5]

The next series of presidential debates did not take place until the 1976 contest between Democrat Jimmy Carter and Republican incumbent Gerald Ford. As had been the case with the earlier debate with Nixon and Kennedy, the first debate between Carter and Ford, which focused on domestic policy, offered insight into the power of television in presidential politics. When a technician accidentally cut off the sound from the stage, both candidates stood, wooden-like for the next 27 minutes, waiting for the sound to return. They were prisoners of television's power, and while the absence of audio was a reason not to continue, the frozen pose said much to those watching. Candidates learned from this debate to have fallback plans in place for technical glitches—sound disappearing or the picture or power going out—and would act much differently. This debate also added to presidential debate history in that it moved from the question and answer format of the 1960 debates to a format in which candidates made opening statements, moderators asked questions to which they could pose follow-ups, and candidates made closing statements.[6]

During the second debate, held in early October, the candidates sparred over matters of international policy. At one point, Max Frankel of the *New York Times* asked President Ford a question about the influence of the Soviet Union on Eastern Europe, to which Ford responded, "There is no Soviet domination of Eastern Europe, and there never will be under a Ford administration." Obviously shocked at this reply, Frankel followed up with, "I'm sorry. Did I understand you to say, sir, that the Soviets are not using Eastern Europe as their own sphere of influence in occupying most of the countries there?" In response, Ford simply offered an elaboration on his earlier answer, declaring, "I don't believe . . . that the Yugoslavians consider themselves dominated by the Soviet Union. I don't believe that the Romanians consider themselves dominated by the Soviet Union. I don't believe that the Poles consider themselves dominated by the Soviet Union. Each of these countries is independent, autonomous, it has its own territorial integrity, and the United States does not concede that those countries are under the domination of the Soviet Union."[7]

As Ford spoke, Carter was shown in a cut-away shot with a big smile and when given the chance to respond, he said that he would like to see Ford "convince the Polish-Americans and the Czech-Americans and the Hungarian-Americans in this country that those countries don't live under the domination and supervision of the Soviet Union behind the Iron Curtain." The next day's stories on the debate focused on Ford's gaffe. Although it later became clear that Ford had meant to say that the United States did not recognize Soviet hegemony in Eastern Europe, the damage was done. The result was a substantial bump in the polls for Carter, who quite rightly felt the debates turned the tide and allowed him to be seen on an equal footing with the sitting president.[8] As with the first Kennedy-Nixon encounter, there was a valuable lesson to be learned: be prepared for any type of question and avoid at all costs speaking off script or message.

*Republican presidential candidate Richard Nixon makes a point
during the first presidential debate, September 26, 1952 (fig. 2)*

AP Images

Incumbent Jimmy Carter listens to Republican challenger Ronald Reagan in their second 1980 debate (fig. 3)

AP Images

Democratic nominee Bill Clinton addresses audience while third party candidate Ross Perot and Republican incumbent George H. W. Bush look on (fig. 4)

AP Images

In the 1980 contest for the White House, in which incumbent President Jimmy Carter faced Republican Ronald Reagan and independent hopeful John Anderson, Carter skipped the first televised debate. His absence may have redounded to the benefit of Reagan, whose exchanges with Anderson convinced many mainstream voters that he was less staunchly conservative than his opponents made him out to be.

Because his poll numbers had dropped, Anderson was not invited to the second debate, and Reagan and Carter had the stage to themselves. In this encounter, Carter accused Reagan of planning to make reductions in Medicare. Reagan, who had been subjected to a number of such charges regarding his social spending plans, simply shook his head and said "There you go again." With this gentle rebuke, Reagan unleashed a new weapon in presidential debates, the one-line quip capable of dominating news coverage for the next few days.[9] *(fig. 3)*

Reagan also took the closing statement of the debate and gave it a new weight when he asked, "Are you better off now than you were four years ago?" This simple question resonated deeply with an electorate plagued by rising interest rates and inflation, and variants have been used by many campaigns since. More important, it became an invaluable lesson in how a carefully coined statement or question can be used to carry the day.[10]

Television debates have become routine in terms of preparation and presentation and often become nothing more than variations of campaign speeches and interviews. There have been, however, a few moments in years following that have come to be a part of electioneering lore in the television age. In 1984, for example, after a very lethargic performance in the first debate, Ronald Reagan came to his second debate with Democratic hopeful Walter Mondale armed with the perfect rejoinder to a public perception that, at age 73, he might be too old for the job. "I want you to know," he announced, "that I will not make age an issue of this campaign. I am not going to exploit, for political purposes, my opponent's youth and inexperience."[11] In taking a prevalent perception and turning it on its head with humor, Reagan added another element to the debate lore.

In the second debate of the 1992 election, which included Democratic hopeful Bill Clinton, incumbent George H. W. Bush, and third party candidate Ross Perot, the most memorable aspect lay in the great difference in the way that Bush and Clinton related to the audience. Taking advantage of the less formal town hall format, Clinton walked toward the audience as he answered one question, breaking the fourth wall of most debate settings and creating an empathetic link with his listeners. *(fig. 4)* In sharp contrast, President Bush was caught looking at his watch during one answer by one of his opponents, sending the message of disengagement. News stories that showed the president removed from everyday life—marveling at something like a grocery store checkout scanner—only amplified his disengagement and doubtless contributed to his defeat.[12]

As televised debates have become an increasingly institutionalized part of presidential campaigning, candidates have learned much from the debate gaffes and successes of their predecessors. They now come to these face-offs much more heavily prepped and ready for almost any question. And in the tradition of that "great communicator" Ronald Reagan, they also often come armed with a few carefully chosen lines intended to make headlines in tomorrow's news.

In 1952, the first commercials for candidates for President were aired. One notable spot for Eisenhower began with an animated bouncing "Ike" button, which transitioned into a cartoon Uncle Sam and a parade of citizens marching while a chorus sang:

> Ike for president, Ike for president,
> Ike for president, Ike for president.
> You like Ike, I like Ike, Everybody likes Ike—for president.
> Bring out the banners, beat the drums,
> We'll take Ike to Washington.[13]

When this kind of ad hit the airways, Eisenhower's Democratic opponent Adlai Stevenson thought that Americans would be shocked by such contempt for their intelligence. "This isn't Ivory soap versus Palmolive," he said.[14]

But if Stevenson harbored some illusion that this Madison Avenue approach to presidential electioneering would not take root, he was dead wrong. Over the next two decades, television promotion of candidates took on characteristics that had much in common with promotional ad campaigns for consumer goods. In 1968, that similarity reached a new high with the slickly orchestrated campaign of Republican hopeful Richard Nixon. As Joe McGinnis richly documented in *The Selling of the President*, the campaign of Richard Nixon took on the flavor of advertising campaigns for consumer goods, including soap.[15] Like it or not, television was changing the rules and dynamics for Presidential campaigns. While there would be notable examples for each campaign, three ads stand out for their dramatic use of the power of television.

In 1964, intending to transform Republican hopeful Barry Goldwater into a wild-eyed anti-communist radical capable of drawing this country into a nuclear holocaust, the supporters of his Democratic opponent, incumbent Lyndon B. Johnson, unveiled an ad that has become known as "The Daisy Girl." *(fig. 5)* In it, a little girl is standing in a field, plucking petals off of a daisy, counting each one slowly. "One, two, three, four, five, seven, six, six, eight, nine, nine. . . ." The camera zooms in to her face and a deep male voice says: "Ten, nine, eight, seven, six, five, four, three, two, one, zero." As the screen turns black and the sound of an exploding bomb is heard and a mushroom cloud appears, President Johnson intones: "These are the stakes: To make a world in which all of God's children can live, or to go into the darkness. We must either love each other, or we must die."[16]

As soon as the ad aired, the Johnson campaign was deluged with angry criticism for using the threat of nuclear war for partisan ends. In light of the criticism, the ad was run only once. But in a perverse way, it had been a success. The point had been made and the news media reinforced it by repeating and recycling the story for days to come.

For many students of political advertising, "The Daisy Girl" is one of the definitive political commercials of all time. Much of its power lay in the juxtaposition of an innocent young girl plucking daisy petals and the deployment of the most fearsome weapon known to mankind. The message each viewer took away was informed in part by what he or she brought to the commercial. For viewers that evening in 1964, the Cuban Missile Crisis was less than two years past and the Cold War seemed to be intensifying by the month. And presidential campaigners learned a valuable lesson—the most effective message is often not told just with what

*Images from
the "Daisy Girl"
television
commercial, 1964
(fig. 5)*

Museum of the Moving Image

Images from "Morning in America" advertising campaign, 1984 (fig. 6)

Museum of the Moving Image